PENROE:
in another field
without time

By David Bosselmann
with Barbara Krause

www.Penroe.net

Library of Congress Cataloguing-in-Publication Data has been applied for.

FIRST EDITION

ISBN 978-0-9909654-0-4

SPIRITUAL/POETRY/ MIND BODY

Dedication

This tribute is dedicated to Mac and Helen Walker, Penny's parents, and to Rosie Hacker Folwell, Kay Lindenbaum Crane, Jan Bach and the Forrest-Strawn-Wing Class of 1953, all of whom supported and influenced Penny during her formative years.

Acknowledgments

On the day of Penny's Memorial Service, January 19, 2008, an idea came to me to write her biography as a way to honor her. At the time, I did not fully envision the extent of the project and had no idea that it would morph into a much broader work. I also did not realize how healing this work would be for me or how it led to new, lasting friendships.

I am immensely grateful for the help of so many friends and acquaintances of Penny and others in the production of this work. I am especially thankful for the guidance and creative ideas of my friend, Kirsten Johnson, who led me to my editor and co-author, Barbara Krause. Kirsten also reviewed the draft manuscript.

That I found Barbara to lead our work seems a miracle to me, certainly serendipitous at the very least. Barbara put her heart and soul into this project, not to mention countless hours of research and drafting. I have been deeply touched by her dedication and spirit. Our working relationship has been the best imaginable. I also much appreciate the creative contributions of Barbara's husband, Paul Krause, who designed the layout and covers of the book. Also, a special thanks goes to Rita Ann Powell, creator of the book's website, www.Penroe.net.

I appreciate the time and efforts of my friends, Jo Bolte and Al Naylor, who also reviewed the draft manuscript, offering valuable critiques. I thank Jan Bach, Penny's lifelong friend, for sharing many fond memories of Penny and for his work in critiquing the draft manuscript. I also thank Judy Brown-Wescott for her review of the draft manuscript.

Many of Penny's friends and acquaintances generously offered their time for interviews and follow up questions. Special thanks go to Rosie Hacker

Folwell, Penny's childhood friend from Illinois, and to Penny's third cousin, David Franklin. I also greatly appreciate the time and cooperation of many of Penny's high school friends including Kay Lindenbaum Crane, Mary Honegger Edinger, Beverly Crouch Haag, John Honegger, Rita Keeley Kohlman, Beth Tomlinson Maier, Neil McLoughlin, Marlene Shive Moore, Ed Schrof, and Marilyn Metz Wyllie.

Others who contributed significantly to this work were Joan Brunkow Ainsley, Karen Biddle Davis, and Judy Brunkow Glasford, Penny's college classmates; Wally Faster, Penny's first husband; and from her life in Minnesota: Connie Bell, Deborah Cheney, Lynn Cox, Marylee Hardenbergh, Libby Hazen, Reverend Robert Hudnut, Leslie Whittles Marble, Wendy Morris, Reverend James Newby, Kate Gardos Reid, Roxanna Rutter, and Susan Simpson. Heartfelt gratitude goes to each of you.

Contents

Introduction

A respite, this captivating fusion of poetry, memoir, and biography reflects the spirit of Penny Walker Bosselmann. The narrative holds space for readers to see beyond their circumstances. Originally a linear biography, the work quickly evidenced a mind of its own. Six notebooks of poetry, numerous journal entries and private diaries echoed a richness that could not be denied. Significant additions, these enhancements created an open invitation for appreciation of nature, a profound awareness of beauty and joy, and honest reflection.

Described as a nature mystic by one who knew her well, Penny invites readers to become aware of how nature can speak to them directly. Penny particularly loved the nature poetry of Mary Oliver, as supported by numerous underlined passages. Besides the influence of nature, Penny was shaped by the values of a small, Illinois town; by a host of characters; by fate; and by questions. Penny bares her soul.

Inventive interpretation presents ordinary concepts to readers in an extraordinary way. The predominant narrator in the first half of the book is Penny's husband, David. To echo her mystical spirit and complement the symbolism in her work, later chapters use creative voices to continue the nature mystic theme. Artistic layouts of these same chapters sharpen contrasts, yet soften realities.

Chapter Nine presents a repartee between David and the writing of Penny. Chapter Ten illustrates Penny's observations about death; these observations spark further suppositions about how to live life more fully. Chapter Eleven is a monologue on the human condition, shaped by the findings of a famous psychiatrist's interviews. Chapter Twelve completes the narrative and balances harsh medical facts with Penny's inner, animal spirit voice. Response is immediate.

Imagining Penny as a friend, sharing conversation across the table, readers embark on a comfortable and engaging love affair with words. Ideas make their way inwardly and quietly settle into the depths of the bones, ready to be contemplated and savored.

Letter to Readers

Penny Walker Bosselmann explored the mysteries of relationships, nature, and spirituality as she listened to her spirit, observed details, and reflected on perceptions of life. Becoming one with nature showed her how to live.

> Pearls falling everywhere,
> more than a king's ransom
> on the grass
>
> and loud as the voices
> of his court
> and it's a good thing.
>
> Trees behind the house,
> as hungry as we are
> for bread.
>
> Roots opening beneath me,
> I hear them
> humming.
>
> These low grey clouds
> run across the sky
> clapping their hands
>
> and all is changed as though a child had been born.
>
> "Rain"
> September 20, 2004

Rain, like words, is transformative. Both impact thoughts, environment, and growth. Both show wisdom in timing and delivery. Both witness miracles. Penny understood the connection between words and the natural world. Her wish for readers is that they take time to find beauty in all circumstances. In doing so, they open their hearts to wisdom and begin to trust in something greater than themselves.

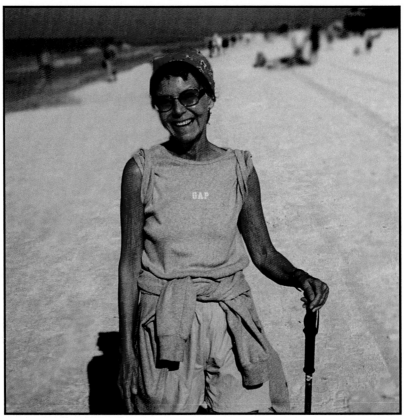

Penny Walker Bosselmann

Penny's Pearls

> ➤ Connect deeply with people. Go to nature and your Higher Power, and they will speak directly to you. Love life because love is magical.

> ➤ Be present as much as possible to all that is happening. Notice the subtle beauty all around you; delight in and appreciate it. Work to protect it.

> ➤ Engage in all that you find nurturing. But don't over-engage. Keep your boundaries.

> ➤ Laugh. Laugh at yourself. Laugh at life and try to make others laugh.

> ➤ Don't expect to find clear answers to the big questions about life. Be content with the mysteries, live the questions.

A priest[1] I know talks about the stars—
how they are born and die as we do
and are at their most beautiful as they die—
and that their changing beauty
remains a mystery.

I know that all mysteries are fluid
like this lavender light in the woods
I watch as I stand by our old white house
waiting for the stars to be born into the sky.

Christmas Collection
2007

This was Penny's final holiday poem. Although she wrote innumerable poems and journal entries to chronicle the wonder and awe she found in all things, it is the *Christmas Collection* of annual poems that friends and family members most revere. For forty years she chose to hand write her poems on exquisite paper, adamantly refusing the conveniences of modern technology. Her heart spoke.

So my dear David, here you are at your fortieth year --
your fortieth birthday, according to John Updike
the midpoint of your life,
and what does it all mean?
Perhaps the meaning is in the simple living of your days
in communion and community with those you love
and with your own spirit.
Perhaps the meaning
is in appreciating the mystery of it all.

Love, Penny

Diary entry
July 8, 1982

Chapter 1
My Pen and Our Love

"Bro, you've got horseshit boundaries," she told me many times. "I know, Penroe," I would say, "but I think I'm doing better." It was one of the few differences between us, and we used it to our advantage.

Pen knew who she was and what she wanted. She was very clear about that. She had little difficulty saying "no" and would tell solicitors that she did not appreciate their using the telephone or coming to our door to intrude on her day. When the unwelcomed knocked, Pen handled the infringement. On the other hand, when we wanted to say "no" to a friend's invitation, Pen would ask me to deal with it. As a habitual conflict avoider, I became very skilled at refusal in a way that was not offensive. Our relationship wasn't always that defined, although we did adopt fairly traditional roles.

Thinking back, it was at St. Luke Presbyterian Church that I first truly noticed Penny, primarily her approachability. She was not intimidating in any way. A delightful, attractive woman who was intuitive and had a sense of humor, she did have a shyness about her that my personality mirrored. Even so, it was unlikely that we would be more than acquaintances. I wasn't looking for a relationship; I just wanted to move on with my life. Shift happens. No one would have imagined that a well-educated, not bad-looking, 6′4″ financial planner would connect with this petite woman.

Early on there was a unique attraction between us. We were aware of being alike in many aspects. Penny wore very out-of-style, cat-eyed glasses and drove an ordinary, older model economy car. Likewise, I valued frugality and simplicity. I remember telling a female friend over coffee that I thought Penny was "a diamond in the rough," and that her wisdom and strength made me a better person.

Being a processor of information, I marveled, in hindsight, about how I was already discovering my true nature. Penny had come through a divorce, and I was headed in that direction. Deeply embedded in me was a charge to become more transparent, to experience an emotional connection, and to grow in love. It was miraculous that I found this knowledge just as I was ready to receive it. Spending time with Penny was the beginning of a new foundation. Like many in their late thirties and early forties, I believed that my purpose was to fulfill the responsibilities of family and home. Depth of relationships was elusive. Getting to know Penny helped me to recognize the complexity of people and, for the first time, I understood the importance of substance in relationships.

In the early years of our relationship, I called her "Pen" and she called me David or "Bos," a nickname from college. After a few years, my son, Chris, started calling me "Budroe," the name of a professional wrestler he picked up from television. Then for some silly reason, we added "roe" to every family member's first name. "Pen" became "Penroe," "Bos" became "Bosroe," and my brother, Steve, became "Steveroe." Pen eventually shortened my name to "Bro," yet I kept using "Penroe."

I had no idea how lucky I was when Penny, who loved singing, wrote about nature and used movement and verbal therapy to help others understand their feelings, fell in love with me early in our courtship. Even though she was classy in that she was educated, appreciated the arts, knew how to dress and understood social etiquette, she had no airs about her, no pretenses.

Penny was nonjudgmental and a free thinker. Even the simplest of directives—wearing name tags—caused her to rebel because she believed that people should focus on the distinctiveness of others through meaningful conversations. A name tag was but a surface means of knowing someone. She held the same beliefs about dress and the righteous games people play to advance their social positions or prestige in a company. In her mind, changing lyrics of old hymns to make them gender neutral and politically correct seemed nothing short of manipulation. She wanted to discover and sustain the basic essence of things.

Traditions mattered to her. I enjoyed a quality of child innocence about her that became particularly evident at Christmas time when she really got into the spirit. Enjoying the atmosphere as we strolled the silver- and gold-gilded halls of The Galleria in Edina, we smiled at a pianist who was playing holiday carols. Soon I heard Pen's voice. I began singing and, before long, another couple joined in. No one cared that we were in the middle of a shopping center. We also ventured annually to see a small tree with white lights located on a land spit by Lake Minnetonka on Ferndale Road. This reflection echoed the perfect simple beauty and elegance of the season.

Holidays also meant carrying out special customs. Penny enjoyed making God's Eyes, Native American symbols that represented the power to see and understand things unknown.[1] Other Easter customs were important to her like decorating Easter baskets and hiding them. Well into her adult years, Karen, Penny's daughter, and I would awaken to find a trail of jellybeans that began at our bedroom doors. We followed the candy path, "surprised" when we discovered our baskets.

Gender equality was important to Penny and to me. In particular, it irked her to hear service providers, who came to our home, ask me questions that she easily could have answered. She did not accept the "good ol' boys' club" approach and was discerning in when to make her feelings known. Neither did Penny push gender equality to extremes; she was satisfied to be the chief homemaker throughout our marriage. Yet, when it came to decisions involving my children, especially regarding finances and visiting arrangements, she did not hold back. I accepted her input, even though I chose not to enter into decisions regarding her children.

In certain situations, she was not afraid to confront people when upset with them. I remember being at the receiving end of her anger when I was twenty minutes late to pick her up from the hospital after hip replacement surgery. Understandably, she was very eager to leave that environment.

...that she knew her truth and lived it

Fuming over my tardiness, she unmercifully harangued me in front of one of the nurses. The incident embarrassed me, but that was my Pen, and I understood her feelings.

Penny felt strongly about following through on commitments and expected the same from others. She would often get angry with service people who didn't show up as they had promised. When that happened, I knew there would be hell to pay. I almost felt sorry for them. Additionally, when she felt that her security was being threatened or someone was condescending toward her, she could come across as being tough and inflexible. When she felt most vulnerable, she tightened. That was her defense against intimidation.

Extremely direct and honest about her feelings, Penny expected the same from others. Profanity was a style element she sometimes used to make a point, with the impact of possibly alienating people or jolting them to new insights. I remember her once using the "f" word to make a point about race. We were in the church choir room with four other men. I was the only one who flinched. Penny believed that society should value the gifts of each person. A well-finessed profanity carried with it the statement: This is who I am, and if you don't like it, deal with it. I loved that she knew her truth and lived it.

The more time I spent with her, the more I realized that underneath her occasionally cantankerous exterior was a softness, a very kind and gentle being, a person of grace who cared deeply about those who were vulnerable, especially animals. Likewise, Pen's commitment to our relationship was one of complete loyalty. I never doubted her in any way. She loved and supported me with all of her being and I, in turn, was totally committed to her. We did everything together. I don't know how many times she told me, "Bro, I just love hanging out together."

Her smile, a landmark characteristic, radiated an uplifting presence. "Bro, do you feel like singing?" she'd say with a grin, asking during times she *knew* that singing was the last thing in the world I would want to do. She loved being playful and silly and could be so damned funny. There were occasions when we attended social events that were less than stimulating. With a straight face and poignant eyes, she would offer her classic line: "Are we having fun yet, Bro?"

Pen was my entertainer...

Pronunciation of words became a source of humor between us. Occasionally, Penny would mispronounce the name of a person, place or concept, and the game was on. I would say, "We'll get all the way to Lake Saganaga before lunch." Pen might say, "OK, Bro. Before lunch, we'll get all the way to Lake Sagatoga." I would say, "No, Penroe, it's not Sagatoga, it's Saganaga. Say, SA-GA-NA-GA." Immediately Pen would pretend to say Saganaga, but intentionally be unable to get out the syllables. After watching her funny expressions in her phony attempt to spit out the word, I would finally say, "Never mind, Penroe," and both of us would have a good chuckle. Pen was my entertainer with her funny comments, gestures, and expressions. As the straight man, I set her up, so we both had a good laugh.

A poet and writer, Penny often imagined herself as nature, to feel what it might be like to be an animal, a tree, or weather—to think as nature might, or to experience humor in its actions. Her contemplative writing was sculpted from uncommon experiences with nature. An animal lover and protector, Penny wrote about her longtime feline companion.

My cat, Lamb Chop,
loves John Updike.
To my knowledge,
she has never met him.

She has never
mentioned his
Pulitzer Prizes or
literary works.

Yet, this morning
in the early light,
I found her stretched out
on COLLECTED POEMS-1953-1993.

As I watched,
she rose, elegant
as a queen,
reached her front

paws down
and began
to lick.

She licked that book
hard and long.
Well, one loves
what one loves.

When I
took it away,
(in its great dampness),
she sat up
and turned
her green eyes
full in my face,
then left the room.

How to console her?
Even tuna is
a sorry meal once
you've licked John Updike.

"My Cat and John Updike"
April 25, 2002

The mist of a bog, dismissed by many, received acknowledgment and appreciation for its role in nature. Penny's imagination brought a different perspective to its wetness and singular qualities.

Mist comes from nowhere,
settles like a lace shawl
over the marsh.
Trees around the edge
are sentinels but have no way to
hold back the mist,
which advances everywhere.
To my eye, the marsh is only
a small island, a postage

stamp from a grey country
no one has ever heard of.

But I know the importance of what I
cannot see.
I know it is larger than even
      a giant marsh animal.
And I know the mist as it
      settles softly here for sleep.
I know the mist will not stay.

"Mist"
February 6, 1998

Once   when hiking with our friends, Kirsten and Jay Johnson, we accidentally came upon a rare and magical gathering of monarch butterflies in Carver Park, Hennepin County, Minnesota. These ethereal bearers of hope were preparing for their nearly 3000-mile migration to California or Mexico.[2] Penny shared the magnificence of the moment.

Here is the cast of characters:
      this mysterious sky
      like a giant blue hat
      pulled over the head
      of the earth—

      and this field
      clear and grandly spacious,
      a suitable set.

      This borrowed jacket,
      Too big for my body
      but rooms to hide these
      brightly colored birds
      who will enter on cue.

The minor characters:
      stands of goldenrod,
      bright gold of kings—

tall and waving grass
and crickets and mice.

All cleverly disguised as
themselves —
and things unseen
like wind waiting (for a cue) —
her entrance.

Now enters:
the main attraction
the cash cow
that which puts even
spaciousness to shame.

Swelling, sparkling, swarming
in this September sun —
orange as pumpkins —
coming in clouds and herds
and millions —
on the brown path
on the goldenrod
in the blue sky.

(And now, the wind's cue)
Applause!

Do you know what you carry inside?
Can you speak it?
Can you rise in the morning
light wearing your own beauty?

"Monarchs"
April 8, 2002

Monarchs, Carver Park Reserve; Victoria, Minnesota

Rising every morning at 4 A.M., Penny ran four miles in our neighborhood and finished her workout by driving to The Marsh, a fitness center a few miles from our home, to swim laps that added another half mile to her routine. Observing the smallest detail of nature, she reflected on life:

> On summer mornings,
>> my habit,
>> to watch the marsh, its movement which
>> I match with my
>> own as best I can,
>> hoping to slow and deepen
>> enough to see what
>> is there; …

> "Sitting III-Receiving as an Exercise"
> July 1, 1997

I introduced her to the North Shore of Lake Superior, near Grand Marais, where we claimed a favorite inlet—Paradise Beach—as our refuge from the world. The rich memories of our visits there inspired Penny.

> Both times I have married
>> I married for love but
>> the second time, oh, the second
>> time is like a patch of purple
>> crocuses a person might
>> chance upon, blooming right
>> out of the February snow.

>> It is like a small box with
>> a bow, wrapped in fuchsia tissue
>> which I mistakenly find on
>> the floor of a closet. I
>> do not open it but wonder
>> if it holds those small, white
>> perfectly round stones I
>> have watched your long fingers
>> pick out of the blue lake,
>> summer after summer.

Paradise Beach on Lake Superior; ten miles northeast of Grand
Marais, Minnesota

And it is like the body
    of the beach itself with no
    beginning and maybe no end.
I am uncharacteristically silent
    with these thoughts, without
    questions or answers. I
    am the fish swimming, not needing
    to understand the water.

"Meditation"
February 12, 1997

In the later years of life, Penny's favorite inspiration was the ocean beach at Siesta Key, Florida. In the final stanza from "The Sea—Siesta Key, Florida," 2002, she wrote, "This morning, I give the sea whatever it wants of me, and the sea gives it back in a new form, as love does."

Penny was a very spiritual person and found spiritual nurturance and reassurance in the beauty of nature. She so appreciated, respected and even revered the miracle of creation in all of its forms. Whether alone in nature, exploring its spontaneous gifts, or walking hand-in-hand with me, she was happy and contented. Reverend Dr. James Newby, formerly of Wayzata Community Church, Wayzata, Minnesota, referred to Penny as a "nature mystic." He understood how she resonated with nature, a way to understand God.

Big, slow, sloppy
come down, come down,
give gravity
its due.

Heavy and light,
like all mysteries,
all lie down together --

Line of trees fades
like half memories of old loves.

The snow is a million white
horses running.

Such serious beauty.

"March Snow"
March 14, 2001

Reverend Casey Alexander commented, "…it is certainly true that Penny was a poet of life as surely as of words. She had rhythm and rhyme in abundance. There was lilt and vigor and surprise and satisfaction that passed from her life to mine, just in knowing her."

Penny required that her friendships be relationships of depth; she had little time for superficial connections. When I started spending more time with Penny, I noticed that she freely offered advice to those she held most dear. "Penny is very wise," once commented Reverend Sally Hill, our minister at the time. She felt that Penny's poetry honored the wisdom of oneness and the grandeur of mature love, relationships that grew singularly, unfolding graciously.

> I cut a ripe avocado
> in half, work carefully
> around the pit with my knife
> lay the quarter-moons
>
> on wheat bread
> and we eat.
> We are silent.
>
> We have grown more silent
> over the years because
> the words have become
> little pieces of confetti
> and the best part of any party
> is when it is over
> and we are on the porch
> in the warm summer night
>
> watching the mellow moon,
> listening to the dark.

"What Has Happened"
May 26, 2005

Penny believed that love and falling in love were magical, evidence of God's presence in our lives. She believed strongly in the importance of love and that our love for each other could never be taken away, that it would transcend our physical deaths. In one of her books, I found the following Garrison Keillor quote, in which I interpreted "wasted" to mean "lost":

"Nothing you do for love is ever wasted."

It was only some years after our marriage that I began to realize what I had in my mate. Although the relationship was sometimes difficult for me in the early years, I came to appreciate the daring hold Penny had on me. I valued her complexities and depth, her antics and humor. She was exactly the right person for me.

At our cores, Penny and I understood each other. We grew in trust and acceptance of each other's imperfections. We laughed more, truly enjoyed being together, and loved deeply. My endearing Penroe made my heart sing for twenty-five years. In recalling those memories and blessings, I turned to her favorite book, THE LITTLE PRINCE, and, at once, understood the wise fox when he said,

"It is only with the heart that one can see rightly;
what is essential is invisible to the eye."[3]

What is essential?
Loving and being loved.
A knowing, or peace of mind.
An environment that allows the true self to flourish.
Happiness generated within.
Respect.

And questions. Penny believed it was vital for people to live their questions...to explore answers without expectation of timing. Ever-present questions became one of Penny's signature attributes.

My neighbor
carries large pails of water
to the daisies
in front of his house,
the serene shade plants in back.

He does not hurry
the way one does not hurry
large animals.
He does not speak
but smiles.

What does it take to be happy?
walking by water?
money in the mail?
coffee with cream, hot or iced?
Is it being inside out in the world
Or outside in?

Does it grow like the grass,
out of silence?

"Questions about Happiness"
May 20, 2005

I could always count on Penny to ask difficult questions. She loved questions and loved what poet Rilke wrote about questions in Letters to a Young Poet.

> "'I would like to beg you Sir, as well as I can, to have patience with everything unresolved in your heart and to try to love the questions themselves as if they were locked rooms or books written in a very foreign language. Don't search for the answers, which could not be given to you now, because you would not be able to live them. And the point is to live everything. Live the questions now. Perhaps then, someday far in the future, you will gradually, without even noticing it, live your way into the answer.'"[1]

Memorial Message, excerpt
Reverend Dr. James R. Newby
January 19, 2008

Chapter 2
Penny's Quest

Observing, questioning and probing came naturally to Penny. As an only child whose parents moved often, she learned that timely posed questions met with little resistance. At four and one-half years of age, "May I go down the block to the Post Office to see Uncle Harry, pleeease?" generally received a favorable answer if asked after lunch rather than before breakfast. Uncle Harry, postmaster general in Forrest, Illinois, had a soft spot for Penny and looked forward to her visits.

She also learned that polite perseverance, sprinkled with patience, endeared her to her mother: ask for something only twice, with no whining. Evolving questions set Penny's feet on a path where she increasingly turned to nature as it became a caring companion of constancy and delight. She learned to understand the world around her under its guidance.

As she took on years, some of her questions teased people; other questions gave them pause to think. Regardless, her questions did not go unnoticed. Observations and analyses of people, animals, and circumstances flowed into her writings. Penny's targeted words and poet's eye awakened many to their truths.

> On Friday
>> owl flies out of the woods
>> like a swift brown cloud,
>
>> lights on near-tree.
>> He's clearly
>> of the ruling class
>
>> and knows a great forgetting.
>> All day — was silent
>> as a monk, but
>
>> in the deeper dark
>> I saw him crouch
>> and fly.
>
>> I heard him
>> ask his
>> only question.
>
>> (When owls call,
>> who listens?)
>
> "Owl"
> June 25, 2003

Her writing offered perspective on events and relationships observed through experience and interpreted through nature. She wanted people to know that no circumstance was insurmountable. Penny intended her poetry and journal entries to spread joy and beauty. She felt camaraderie with those who were struggling in any way and wanted them to feel hope and personal empowerment through her words.

He's clearly of the ruling class

From the time Penny first kept a journal at eleven, she recognized that questions represented the "more" she had always wanted to know, the "more" that was missing unless she asked for it, the "more" that intrigued her over time, shaping her life, and ultimately the lives of others. From childhood, she never tired of her quest, driven by curiosity and imagination.

The land is dark and makes no sound.
A child walks across the fields.
He is looking for something.
Is it in the grass of the fields,
        the warm dirt that holds
        the grass?
Is it in the stars stretching
        across the fields?
It does not matter. All places
        are magic.

The snow begins.
Child, be inside me.
Be inside those I love.

Christmas Collection
1979

On my hand,
a tickle.
For you, my hand
is a warm rock.

You nod your gray,
pebble eyes away,
flick see-through wings,
green as the woods

you came from.
I am full of questions.
Where do you go at night?

Do you live for a day

or a week, these human concerns.
Then I just wait
and love your sunning

yourself on my hand.
Then you rise
like a tiny helicopter
and move into the blue morning.

"Dragon Fly"
August 19, 2003

There is the sense of coming near,
yet neither holding nor grasping.
It is like light to a forest.

There may be an instrument
to consult concerning direction,
But I find it to be invisible.

To ask,
To remember,
To embrace the sweet madness
drawn out of a man as his breath.
Do we follow or are we pursued?

"Follow"
Christmas Collection, 1970

As if to indelibly mark in her memory, Penny underlined in her journal
these excerpts from T.S. Eliot:

...We shall not cease from exploration
And the end of all our exploring
Will be to arrive where we started
And know the place for the first time.
Through the unknown, unremembered gate

When the last of earth left to discover
Is that which was the beginning;
...And all shall be well and
All manner of thing shall be well
When the tongues of flame are in-folded
Into the crowned knot of fire
And the fire and the rose are one.[2]

... And all shall be well ...

It is 1948 and I am skating
        on a creek in Illinois.
        It is twilight.
Only my friend,
        my best friend, and I are
        skating down this creek.
As the creek bends, it empties
        into the pink sky—
        The day dies.

We don't want to go home,
        want to skate this creek all
        the way to Canada or Russia—
        want to skate into the pink
        sky forever.
There is such solemn silence
        around us.
Only the swish of skates on ice makes sound.

The next year, my friend,
        my best friend, dies.
She dies from a disease that
        silently consumes her 12 year old body.
She dies and none of us
        can stop her.

It is snowing this morning—
        light snow falling straight down,
        no wind.
In the grey light, I walk to the
        edge of the woods, put fresh
        corn and seeds for the animals
        in the feeder.
I say nothing.
It is completely still except for the
        crunch of my boots in the snow.
It is clear.
        The bond is silence.

"On Saying Nothing"
February 27, 1996

Chapter 3
Why?

Grandma Mazella Monroe Clark had a habit of leaving her husband and daughter whenever the spirit moved her and would stay away from home for long periods of time. A compromised childhood began early for Helen Clark, Penny's mother. Once, after yet another of Mazella's extended stays away from home, Grandpa Fred Clark asked, "Helen, should we take back your mother, Mazella?" Helen's reply, "No!"

At a relatively young age, Helen was taken to Forrest, Illinois, to live with her great aunt and uncle, Hazel and Harry Franklin. They raised her. As an adult, she found employment as a telephone operator. Later Helen moved to Chicago where she worked as a law librarian.

Helen presumably met Penny's father, Malcolm (Mac) Walker, while she was working in Chicago where he was working for Standard Oil. An entry from the Walker family Bible, a traditional place where families of this era kept records of births, marriages and deaths, confirmed that they married in Chicago on June 20, 1929. Their only child, a daughter, was born on July 4, 1935, in Mason City, Iowa. Bliss Walker was the name on her birth certificate, yet at some time in her childhood, she became known as "Penny." Perhaps it had something to do with using one of the syllables from "In-de-pen-dence," in honor of her birth date.

Rosie Hacker Folwell, Penny's best childhood friend, knew her as Penny Bliss Walker, yet believed her full name was Independence Bliss Walker. Rosie called her Independence; so did Great Aunt Hazel Franklin. Yet, "Changing her name to 'Penny' sounds like something Mac would have done. Her mother, Helen, was more formal about things, but Mac was laid back somewhat," said Rosie. This was part of the mystery of Penny.

Penny's anxiety about change most likely began with the relocations associated with her father's work. With the intent of adding stability to their lives, Helen took Penny to visit their Forrest relatives quite often. In 1940, Mac, Helen, and Penny moved to Dallas, Texas. Evenings of stifling heat were etched in Penny's memory: her family of three often slept in their backyard with only the blessing of air movement.

Penny and Mac had a special bond. Penny told me that she loved her father and knew that he loved her. She counted on his consistent presence and encouragement.

The day I got my first pair of patent leather shoes was the day before my birthday. I was five, and we lived in Dallas. My mother had been very uncertain of the practicality of such a purchase. To her, the shoes were gold-gilded, diamond studded wedgies, but I pleaded at the shoe store. After all, they were my birthday present. My mother had suggested a baby doll whose eyes opened and closed. This was interesting, but could not compare with the shiny, black shoes with slender black straps and tiny, silver buckles.

When we got home, I put the shoes on. I took off my shorts and tee shirt and put on the white polka dotted dress purchased for my birthday party. I walked downstairs. It was almost time for dinner, and I knew my father would be home soon. I could hardly wait to show him the shoes. The minute he was in the door, I pointed to my shoes.

"Beautiful," he said. "Your shoes are beautiful, and you look like a princess."

Over some objections from my mother, I was allowed to wear the shoes to supper, though I had to change back to my shorts and tee. All during supper I felt the soft patent leather gently holding my feet.

While my mother and father were talking, I slipped away from the table and went to our screened porch in the back of the house. There was no furniture on the porch in preparation for my party the next afternoon. The Texas sun had set and the sounds of twilight were all around me. I stood for a moment, smelling the flowers growing by the porch. I watched the lavender sky deepen its colors.

Then I remembered the shoes. I shifted my weight from one foot to the other and back again. I began to listen to the cricket music the twilight was making. I started to dance. Slowly my body began to move to the rhythm of crickets and sounds of twilight. The shiny, black shoes were forgotten.

That was the first time I knew I loved being a girl.

"Some Things Really Matter"
October 9, 1996

In the summers, beginning when Penny was five, Mac would travel to Forrest with his daughter and wife to visit the Franklin relatives. These visits anchored Penny. Sometimes she would stay for several weeks and sometimes for the entire summer. On some trips, Penny brought along her beloved dog, Gussie, her constant shadow.

Mac was described as "very nice; kind, but quiet; a gentleman" by those Forrest residents who knew him. He often could be seen sitting on a lawn chair, reading, absorbing the warmth of the golden rays that basted his skin.

As for Penny, townspeople remembered hearing her voice as they walked past the windows of the Franklins' home. This combination of talent, plus a bit of nonconformity — after all, she *did* have some of Grandma Mazella's maverick genes — became the mystery that differentiated Penny. Soon the Walker family moved to Long Island, New York.

> …The pattern for moving was always the same.
> My father and mother would go ahead

Penny

Mac

29

and look for a house. I would stay with my
great aunt and her family and go to school in
the town where they lived. When my parents
found a house, they would send for me. I
am not sure why we moved so often, but my
mother said my father wanted to. My father
has always been a great mystery to me.

"Closing a House," excerpt
July 7, 1982

To an elementary-school-aged child with few cares, only the present
moment truly mattered. Penny viewed her parents as being perfect and
always knowing what to do.

I am six, and it is the summer of 1941. It's a hot
July Saturday on Long Island, and my father
and I head for the beach, Jones Beach. He jerks
the car forward through the traffic. Even in the
front seat, I feel a little sick.

It's a glorious day at the beach — sunny, hot,
stiff wind off the ocean. Gulls call, dive close to
the water, rise again like so many spirits. It is
quiet, too early for most.

My father sits on an old red blanket, reading.
I am close to the water, making structures in
sand. Soon restlessness overcomes my father.
He takes my hand, leads me into the water.
Waves rise up against our legs. I jump over
them easily.

Deeper now in the water, my father is chest
high. He holds me high on his chest, my legs
dangling. He jumps each wave with precision.
I am moving with the rhythm of a giant
horse. Sun is on my face, and I am giddy with
pleasure.

Suddenly, my arms and legs are thrashing in the water as I am trying to keep my head up. Waves suck my small body down. I am terrified. Then I feel hands on my sides, lifting me, moving me up to the surface.

I am on the beach, coughing and spitting up water. My father pushes my back down, pressing water out of my lungs. I am breathing hard, lying on the soft, warm sand.

That night, I am fondly tucked into bed. I lie on my side, looking out my windows at the summer stars. They are so beautiful. I think about the warm sand and the water. I think about riding the waves with my father.

I think about falling, falling under the waves, under the water, and I know. I know that everything has changed. My father is not the man he was this morning at breakfast. I am not the same child. I turn again, look at the stars, and wait for sleep.

"Father and I"
August 19, 1996

Mac was a man determined to get ahead. According to several city directories of the time, he worked for at least three different companies during his lifetime, all under the umbrella of sales. Job titles included Sales Promoter for Standard Oil, Minneapolis; Sales Manager for Butler Brothers, a warehouse company that stored goods for Ben Franklin stores, Dallas; and Executive Vice President of Belnap and Thompson, creators of work incentive plans, Chicago. Expensive clothing was his trademark.

The family relocated to Bannockburn, Illinois, a small, upscale village thirty miles north of Chicago. This move seemed to create some consistency and predictability for Penny.

31

> ...I lived in that house for the 3 years just
> before my father died. That was ages 8 through
> 11. The best thing about that house was that we
> lived there for 3 years, the longest we had ever
> stayed in one place.
>
> "Closing a House," excerpt
> July 7, 1987

Penny rarely complained about the paths taken in her life. However, I know she was a happier person when she was surrounded by consistency and predictability. Where would life take her? Several years later, with quick pronouncement, the connection to Forrest would become even more important.

As Penny entered her pre-adolescent years, Mac battled metastatic cancer. I believe that Penny was confused by Mac's illness and subsequent death, especially in contrast to the blossoming of her own life. Mac died in the summer of 1947, at the age of forty-seven. Penny was twelve. "After that," remembered Rosie Hacker, "Penny was different when she came to live in Forrest. She didn't have that innocent girl sensitivity. A funny girl making silly faces, Penny tried hard to make others think she was simply a carefree child. To those of us who knew her well, some of her public image seemed forced. Penny was a wonderful, complicated person."

> ...The night my father died I remember my
> mother waking me and telling me that my
> father had died in the hospital. I remember
> lying in the dark after she had gone downstairs,
> singing a song, partly to myself, partly to my
> father and listening to the voices coming up
> from the living room of that house.
>
> ...My mother and I closed that house, the last
> one where we had all lived together. When we
> were putting everything in packing boxes, I
> remember thinking about my father and that
> dying must be like closing the house of his
> body and going away. ...We will be slow and

quiet as leave-taking cannot be hurried.

"Closing a House," excerpts
July 7, 1982

By August of that summer, Helen had purchased the Forrest Hotel of ten rooms, taking over the entire first floor as their home. Penny's small bedroom was in the northeast corner and housed an upright piano. Today Forrest has restored the hotel as an historic site, offering room rentals, food service, and a gift shop. A portrait of Penny at age eight adorns a wall, close to what was once her room.

Throughout her junior high school years, Penny was curious about her heritage. Learning about the male figures of her lineage gave her roots and eased the longings for her father.

> My great, great grandfather
> whom I knew by reputation
> only, who was many-colored
> as the Texas fireworks
> he loved.
> Was bombast, a
> Methodist preacher who
> rode a horse through small
> towns in Texas, preaching
> the gospels.
>
> His son, my grandfather, sold
> shoes in St. Louis, married
> a psychic, was a small man,
> rosy and bespeckled, silent,
> silver-haired, proper, dapper.
> My memory is of dancing on
> his shoes in a St. Louis
> club when I was six.
>
> My father died young. Some
> said, *All show and no substance.*
> But I don't believe that.

He wanted and bought expensive
things, especially when he
couldn't afford them, worked
hard at what he thought
was success, died when
I was twelve, wanting only
simple things, a quiet
life with my mother and me.

I remember thinking about
being a boy, maybe before
I was born or when I
was very young.
I remember riding the hills on a horse
in the spring green fields
of Ilinois, climbing
the high trees of the woods,
waiting there watching the
stars come out of hiding,
waiting there 'til my father
came and fetched me home.

"A Field of Men"
August, 1996

Later in life, after Penny adopted a son, Tom, she wrote about how her
father and son might have related. I knew that male abandonment was an
issue for Penny. Her time with Mac clearly was cut short. Some difficult
years with Tom in high school tested Penny's deepest instincts.

I am waiting by a tall street light for the bus to pull in.
Tom steps down from the platform,
        walks toward me, smiling.
He seems younger than at our last meeting six months ago.
I hug him, smile back, "Welcome home, Tom."

My father died many years before Tom was born.
He had a smiling, jagged face, was fond of fishing,
        people, private label whiskey.

If he could, he would have waited for Tom.
I miss my father.

I try to unravel the mystery of two men.
They are young foxes, full of their own thick, red fur
     and their own fox tricks.
Both at home in the night woods.

If Tom lives to be 20, I'll be glad.
I will fight for the life of my son.
With fingers and arms, I dig him out of
     the hip-high dirt and rocks.
I take him to a place of large animals,
     animals that move gently on the earth.

And the mystery comes with us.
Where else would it go?
In the evening, the white mare lies down
     on the cool grass, lies down with my son.
She keeps him warm in the frigid night
     under the stars.

"Have You Ever Seen a Stranger?"
April 9, 1996

Mac's memory was precious. His picture was an honored treasure that graced Penny's nightstand all of her days. Recollections of people and events may fade or take on a life of their own, yet by all measure, they unmistakably speak to us.

In a folder marked "Unfinished Work," I found a yellow-lined tablet on which Penny had written a letter to her father, an assignment for a poetry class she had attended. She wrote of her life up to that point. Penny would have been in her early forties.

    Father,
     You would be surprised if you knew how often
     I think of you. Last time I saw you I was twelve
     years old. Now I have a twelve-year-old of my

own, a girl, and a nine-year-old son.

...I am a student again. I studied music (does that surprise you?) for three years in college... got married and then divorced.

...Don't worry about the divorce. I have become very self-sufficient.

...Do you know that the walks we took early Sunday mornings are such suspensions for me? ...The price of life in this dimension is loneliness...It is too bad you died when I was only twelve. We would have had fun together. I am more like you than you can imagine.

Letter, excerpts
October 20, 1978

And, twenty years after that poetry assignment, she again recounted memories of her father. Having long ago passed through the portals of some of the most impressionable years of her life, Penny maintained an outwardly happy and funny façade, perhaps to emulate the characteristics she liked best about her father. Yet, unforgotten grief plummeted to the depths of her heart where it permanently lodged and, during quiet moments, asked "Why?" The safe silence of skating and the deep ache in her heart remained.

...I have been trying to write about my father with very little success, and no wonder. There is very little I remember about him — a few half-remembered events. Even though I remember very few actual events with him, my heart remembers everything. As I write, the tears come and, even at my ripe old age (61), I miss him terribly. It is hard to admit how much I miss him. I do not want to retreat into analysis of this or solutions for the sadness. I think my job is to simply and painfully remember.

Journal entry
August 6, 1996

If
lightning
bugs were
fires, if fires
were fireworks,
if the fourth of July
would fall to November,
we'd warm our hands
at hearth and hold summer in a jar.

"Lightning Bugs"
July, 2004

Chapter 4
Forrest Memories

The Village of Forrest, Illinois, incorporated in 1870, was nestled halfway between Chicago and St. Louis. The site of a Norfolk and Western Railroad interchange, Forrest emerged as a trade center and grain market. By the 1960s, the town turned to agriculture and honored its railroad heritage with an iconic restoration of a red caboose. Forrest is now a vibrant farming community of 1225 residents.

In 1947, Penny's mother envisioned Forrest as a refuge for a single mother raising a daughter. By the end of that summer, she and Penny had become residents. Her roots in Forrest, Helen was able to pursue her business, feeling comfortable in the knowledge that the town would nurture her daughter. Forrest residents described Helen as sophisticated and elegant, a classy dresser, and one who completed her ensemble with a hat. A strong personality, Helen was very much in charge of matters relating to Penny. David Franklin, Penny's third cousin, doesn't remember outward displays of affection between them.

Penny offered notes, written in 2006, on her mother's hotel business.

> Mother was raised by Aunt Hazel for a significant part of her life. There was a strong connection between them. Aunt Hazel would help at the ten-room hotel on occasion,

sometimes standing in for Mother when she was away or ironing sheets on the mangle iron located in the basement. Railroad men, hunters in the November hunting season, and occasional traveling salesmen were patrons [but] never visiting friends or family of the townspeople. It was considered improper hospitality.

Daily and nightly work in the hotel was hard, and my mother was tired much of the time, even with Aunt Hazel's help. An old coal furnace heated the hotel, and my work each day was to shovel coal from the basement bin into the roaring furnace. When Uncle Harry was well enough (he suffered emphysema from years of smoking), he took the large, burned coal deposits, known as clinkers, out of the furnace with giant tongs; otherwise, the job fell to my mother.

Across from the Forrest Hotel, and just a half block away from the Franklins, lived Rosie Hacker Folwell, Penny's favorite childhood playmate. Rosie remembered visiting Uncle Harry at work. A tidy man who methodically wore a bow tie, Harry was driven by details and schedules. Yet when the girls came to see him, time seemed to disappear. His grandson, David Franklin, recalled visits when the girls were invited in through the back door of the Post Office so they could poke their fingers in the crates of baby chicks.

One summer when Penny and Rosie were five and six, they decided to participate in the annual Forrest Fourth of July parade. At that age, Rosie decidedly believed that the parade was a celebration of Penny's birthday, so they had to be part of the festivities. Driven by their love of pets and imagination, they decorated a doll buggy with crepe paper; put Rosie's dog, Spot, in the buggy; and entered the parade.

Rosie and Pen also made dolls out of edible hollyhock flowers and buds.[1] Pen once made two, and Rosie made eight. Penny said, "You don't want eight kids, do you, Hack?" They also mixed mud pies, adding cherries

The Forrest Hotel in Forrest, Illinois

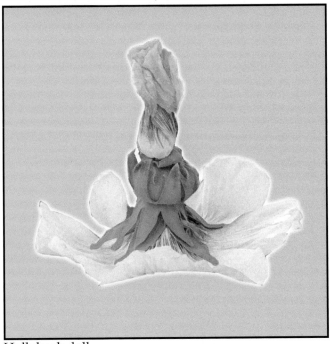

Hollyhock doll

for variety. Apparently the cherries had worms in them, but as Rosie said, "You could never kill a worm around Penny."

"We played dolls during one of Penny's summer visits," remembered Rosie. "I didn't have a doll, so Penny shared hers. After Penny went home and school began, I received a brown box in the mail. Hardly able to contain my excitement at the return address, I carefully opened the wrapping. A doll—my very own doll—lovingly gazed up at me. I will never forget that day. I named the doll Penny Bliss and played with her until she was almost in shreds."

Even then, Penny set up personal boundaries. She took a nap every afternoon—a practice that she continued during the years I knew her. Visitors were asked to wait at home during Penny's naps. Rosie devised a system to time her friend's nap. She and Donna Moulton sat on Donna's front porch swing, listening as Penny sang herself to sleep. About an hour or so later, the girls heard the familiar strains of "Over the Rainbow." They knew it was time to play again.

Another memory was of autograph books—those end-of-school-year, popular legacies of personality and wit. The more silly verses and signatures that could be written on the pages, the better. Rosie remembered reading what Penny wrote in her book and laughing so hard that she nearly wet her pants.

A close friend to Penny during their early teenage years was Beverly Crouch Haag. She remembered walking with Penny the day that the news broke of the Korean War.[2] Beverly said they both wondered, "Where is Korea?" Pen was never much interested in geography.

Sometime later, David Franklin recalled that he walked with Penny and her friends to the railroad yards. They were intrigued by the spectacle of young women exchanging pleasantries and occasional mementos with soldiers whose eager flirting caused them nearly to fall out of the train windows.

Beverly was quite fond of Penny even though Pen would talk her into doing things that, after agreeing, seemed completely beyond Beverly's sensibilities. It was a Methodist Church tradition for youth to deliver

Dear Rosy,   March 13, 1948

I [🚂] cry,
I [🚂] laugh
I [🚂] sign my [♪] graph.

            Penny

yours till
I get my hair warshed   PS that will
                         be pretty
                         long!!!
(dont read alloud)

                    June 21, 1948
                    Forrest, Ill,

Dear Rosa,
  Can't think
Born dumb,
inspiration wont come,
out of ink,
dumb pen
  Best Wishes
Amen !!! !
        !!!!
      Love, Freddie? I do
            Penny

Autographs

the sermon for the Easter Sunrise Service. One year Pen talked Beverly into giving the sermon. As Beverly reached the pulpit in the dawn of that morning, she couldn't find the lectern light and had to address everyone entirely from memory. Pen had a persuasive way about her.

In the fall of 1949, Penny entered her freshman year at Forrest High School. She once confided to me that she felt more comfortable in a small town away from the competition of upscale Bannockburn. Forrest was a special place where Penny could heal and thrive. And thrive, she did.

One of her best friends was Kay Lindenbaum Crane who lived on a farm on the edge of town. With abundant space, Kay's farm was the perfect place to explore and skate on a creek, drive Kay's jeep, and ride horses. It was also the ideal location to build and decorate a class Homecoming float.

> My best friend's farm,
>> only a mile from town,
>> an easy hike, they had
>> horses.
> Her father taught me to
>> saddle and bridle a horse,
>> gave me free access.
> Spring comes early that year
>> on Illinois farms. I am
>> with the horses every
>> afternoon (I bring apples
>> and sometimes sugar cubes from home).
> The cold and snowy months come.
>> I visit the white mare
>> every afternoon. This is
>> the first time I know
>> I love something.
> On this certain January evening,
>> I slip into the barn, light
>> snow coming down. She
>> raises her head. I take
>> the wire brush from its
>> hook, get up on a stool,

and brush her back and neck. She
stands completely still.
I see the snow drift down
through the open barn
door. I rub the white
mare's ankles, brush
her mane.
Its long, white hairs fall to
my feet, silent as loving,
silent as snow.

"White Mare"
August, 1997

Unlike most teenaged girls, Penny wasn't obsessed with her hair. Hair was hair. Yet, in her heart of hearts, there was something that would have made her trade a favorite possession.

…As a child, my own curls
danced around my face, brown.
Hair was nothing much to me unless it was
a dog's or cat's.

But, at 15, I would have given my best sweater, pink
angora, for hair straight as sticks…

"Hair," excerpt
January 8, 2001

Kay described Penny as "a kind of goddess that I was almost in awe of; fun-loving, outgoing, responsible, never got into trouble; and very active in school and the community." Directness in all matters was another one of Penny's strong personality traits. She didn't gossip about others and was not an instigator. Witty, yet not sassy, Penny did have an edge and could be a bit reckless and naïve. Kay believed there was a "kind of imp underneath her good girl image." She relayed the story of the day that Penny borrowed her mother's gray, 1950 luxury Packard. Pen picked up Kay, and they drove to nearby Champaign (about an hour's drive) in thirty-five minutes. Kay's memory registered a distinct eighty-five to

43

ninety miles per hour speedometer reading.

> When I was young,
> the world lived close to me.
> I heard the bells (bells of the Methodist Church, three blocks
> from the Forrest hotel).
>
> Still they call
> over my gathering or dancing,
> weeping or breaking.
>
> For you I love,
> I ask thunder of bells
> through the soft night.
>
> "The Bells"
> *Christmas Collection*, 1971

The 1940s and 1950s were a time of trust and new inventions. After school, Penny and her friends often stopped by the lumberyard, owned by the father of one of Penny's friends, Jan Bach. There, they watched programs on a round-screened TV.

According to Jan, "Favorite programs were *Life with Elizabeth*, starring Betty White and Richard Deacon as her next door neighbor and *Wrestling with Russ*. The memorable part of the wrestling series was Russ's all-purpose clip that ended every program. 'Well, that was really one to write home about, wasn't it?' — regardless of opponent or action. And he thought no one would notice!"

Most summers in Forrest were idyllic, especially for teenagers. Penny loved to sing "God Bless America" and sang it every chance she could, and always on her birthday. Penny was asked to sing at the beginning of the free summer evening movies provided by the city.

For a week during the summers, Penny attended Camp Newaygo[3] which offered twenty-seven acres of horseback riding, swimming, canoeing, and crafts. She looked forward to the annual train trip to the wooded wonderland. Penny continued her association with the camp as a counselor during the summers of her college years.

The kids of Forrest made their own fun. Although some of it was mischievous, it was never intended to harm. Penny and her friends were fully engaged in pinching[4] watermelons from farm fields and exploring deserted farmhouses at night. Frightened by some adventures, Penny's friends could always count on her to lead the way into a dark, scary basement. This explained why Rosie attributed the following characteristics to Penny: first, and foremost, fun loving; then daring; and third, a tomboy.

Most kids worked on area farms and babysat to earn summer money. Penny had two jobs: walking the beans, which meant weeding beans and detasseling the corn.[5] She proudly added money earned from these jobs to her five-dollar-per-week allowance.

> As for the corn fields, think back to childhood, they are there in flat and somber Illinois and I am 15, the only girl in the crew, here to make money, best part-time work in the country. Up at 4:30 A.M., start at 6, bring a lunch, work steady 'til 4. Ride this big, square, hollow thing (a solemn procession). Got no guts, no insides that any respectable animal has.
>
> God, it was hot. My hair was long then and curly — stuffed it under a cap, red. Sweat right through it and my shirt. Sweat dripping down into my face. The salt stings, but it was $5.50 an hour, all mine.
>
> At 4 P.M., into the creek, clothes and shoes on. Into the creek cool with horses and cows close enough to touch, to lean on, to stroke. I wait, hungry and cool, for a ride. Then my mother came. Then I was 60.
>
> "Detasseling the Corn"
> July, 1998

Detasseling the corn

Like any small town in America, Forrest had its share of colorful characters. King of Forrest was Sheriff Bill Doyle and his old pick up truck turned squad car. Making his methodical rounds among those leaning toward bad behavior, he tried to cajole them into choosing the higher road. Lefty Rush, the town character, was a handyman and called all the kids "Sunshine." Hobos, brought into town by passing trains, showed up on doorsteps to seek handouts. Penny loved the laid-back lifestyle of Forrest and the down-to-earth, kindly people.

Certainly recognized by the community, Penny was also held in high esteem by members of the Class of 1953. Consensus was that Penny was "willing to help anyone." In classes at Forrest-Strawn-Wing (FSW), the name given to Forrest High School after the district incorporated two nearby towns, she took a front row seat. Penny was serious about classes and seemed to appreciate why she was there. Activities accompanying her picture in the high school yearbook, *The Tupek*, were National Honor Society member, cheerleader, lead in *Girl Shy*, writer for "The Tonic" school newspaper, and Homecoming Queen.

Penny had a reputation as an independent and profound thinker. Neil McLoughlin, homecoming king their senior year, remembered Penny fondly because she was a girl who made conversation comfortable. Mary Honegger Edinger remembered class discussions where Penny shared ideas and opinions that would spark creative insights.

Penny and Jan Bach, a student two years younger, developed a lifelong friendship through their common interest in music. "One of my fondest memories was the time when Penny agreed to my request to listen to my very first long-play (LP) record,[6] some arrangements of Bach works by Leopold Stokowski. We sat in an empty classroom and played the record on a portable phonograph. I can still see Penny sitting there with her arms folded, transfixed, as she stared into space."

Except for her platonic relationship with Jan Bach, Penny didn't develop lasting relationships with any of the high school boys; however, she did date several of them. One was Ed Schrof, a solid young man, whom Helen really liked. Reportedly, Penny also had a crush on Jimmy Virkler, but ended up dating his brother, Perry. Beverly Crouch Haag offered this information about developments with Perry:

It was a time when Penny had lost interest in dating Perry, yet he decided to give her a holiday gift. Helen, seeing Perry walk through the door of the hotel with a beautifully-wrapped package, had to think fast. Penny did not have a gift for him — why would she? However, hell-bent on avoiding social embarrassment, Helen quickly disappeared, returning with a gift. Much to Penny's embarrassment, it was one of Mac's ties.

Penny also had an interest in parapsychology, and she and her friends experimented by sending telepathic messages to each other. This led to a natural curiosity of séances and the Ouija board.[7] One weekend, Penny invited friends to join her in a session with the Ouija board. The message, "Beware of drugs" was spelled out. This statement was very disturbing to one of the participants who had planned to enroll in nurses' training after high school.

Other social moments provided scandalous enlightenment. Beverly Crouch Haag told of a slumber party held in nearby Strawn. That evening one of the girls revealed to the group that she was no longer a virgin. Beverly said that Penny was shocked and asked so many questions that it made Beverly uncomfortable.

At a later slumber party that Penny hosted at her hotel, Marilyn Metz Wyllie remembered a red-letter evening. The girls had been smoking when Penny's mother knocked on the door. "We threw open the windows to try to get rid of the smoke, while somehow making the cigarettes disappear." Penny was fully engaged, if not leading these activities.

Students looked forward to class trips. Having the superintendent's daughter, Beth Tomlinson Meier, in the ranks provided an extra bonus for Penny's classmates during their senior year. Instead of the usual Chicago destination, the class was able to visit Washington D.C. and New York City where they took a boat tour around Manhattan and the Statue of Liberty.

Additionally, this era was a time when parents could count on local churches to help shape the values of their children.

...My mother insisted that I attend the Methodist Sunday School and church, so Reverend P. Henry Lotz and I ended up together. When he spoke, his voice was as soft as the sound of the mice under our porch. I heard P. Henry Lotz raise his voice only once. I was 15, and he came to the Methodist Youth Fellowship (MYF) group to discuss the dangers of alcohol and smoking.

...Another time I stopped by to see him in the fall of my freshman year of college. He asked me how I liked school. This was the opening I had come for and I spilled over the banks of myself for over an hour. I did this as though he had never been to college, was totally unfamiliar with its challenges and its glories. P. Henry listened quietly.

...Since that time I have learned considerably about my place in the living of things. I have also been acquainted with and even friendly with many preachers, some eloquent, some with fire for the Lord. None have listened so well as P. Henry Lotz or been able to bear the sweetness and kindness of silence.

Journal entry, excerpts
March 15, 1997

It is quiet here in the woods.
I come to keep company with whatever
    of me is most at home with these
    trees, each a story of itself
    and the small animals.
    Mouse and fox-print in the snow
    and what I guess is the sound

of deer beyond the rise
    of the hill.
What I want to tell you now
    cannot be told in words.
Listen with me for the flight of the fox
        and watch for what hides
        beyond the hill.
Now, oh now at last, I begin to know
        that which I cannot see.

Christmas Collection

1978

The man is walking at night
　　or is he dreaming of walking?
At any rate,
　It is dark and he is alone.
　As he walks, he looks up at the dark sky.
　There is a crescent moon and millions of stars.
　Stars ask him questions
　　or does he dream they ask?
　At any rate,
　　he has no answers.
Though this man knows many answers,
　　he has none for these stars.

He walks. He knows he cannot stop walking.
He feels warm wind on his face.
"I feel warm wind on my cheeks," he says.
　　This cannot be a dream!"
He may be right.
At any rate,
　　the wind speaks
　　yet so softly the man cannot
　　hear the words.
But the message is clear.

"Bird's Birthday Poem"
January 28, 1996

Chapter 5
The Articulate Wind

Penny's illustrious high school credentials spoke clearly to the admissions personnel at the University of Illinois (UI), Champaign-Urbana, just fifty miles south of Forrest. Armed with an early acceptance letter, she visited the campus in the spring of her senior year in high school and was fascinated by conversations with women from Alpha Phi Sorority. They relished Pen's amusing facial expressions, fun-loving nature, and sense of humor; she would be a perfect addition to their sorority. Penny's decision to join sorority life the following fall made her initial college year less intimidating and lonely. She had gained an instant family of sisters.

During the second semester of her freshman year, she met the Brunkow twins, Judy and Joan. The three became close friends, almost to the dismay of their Alpha Phi house mother who had a heart-to-heart talk with them about being too clannish. Joan remembered many happy and fun times with Penny, particularly the rendition of a high school cheer: "Beat me, Daddy, eight to the bar. Forrest High School's goin' far."

Penny's music and dramatic arts talents came in handy for sorority ventures. The Alpha Phi's joined with a Jewish fraternity to enter the Spring Carnival Stunt Show, a campus-wide competition. Joan, Judy, and Penny were cheerleaders in the skit that took first place. A year later, Penny's association with the Alpha Phi's was most likely the driving force behind her becoming a runner-up on the UI Homecoming Court. Pen said that it was political.

It was also during that year that Penny met Wally Faster through their involvements in two clubs: Young Women's Christian Association (YWCA) and Young Men's Christian Association (YMCA). Wally was a handsome, well-mannered young man who she believed was a "good catch." They began dating.

During her sophomore year, Penny entered the School of Music, declaring a major in voice. She became close friends with Karen Biddle Davis, a Pi Phi from nearby Bloomington, Illinois. Karen recalled that being part of the School of Music was a humbling experience and believed that Penny must have felt similarly. "She had a rich alto voice and would sing folk songs like 'Black is the Color of My True Love's Hair' and 'The Streets of Laredo.'" Penny's voice and style were distinct. During a church choir rehearsal, the director had asked the female voices to sing a particular phrase. True to her style, Penny sang with gusto. Expecting to hear only high-pitched voices, the director retorted that there should be no male voices singing. What he thought was a male voice had, indeed, come from Penny.

As was her nature, she was curious about activities outside of academia. Penny joined Women's Glee Club, served on the executive council of the Campus YWCA, and served as president of TORCH, a sophomore student honorary group. Based on her first three years of scholarship, leadership, and service, she was awarded membership in Mortar Board.

This distinguished organization, the first female honorary group on campus, recognized senior status women with a GPA of 3.25 or higher. Later this organization became co-ed.

One summer Penny served as a counselor to inner city girls at a Y camp near Central Valley, New York. In a letter to Jan Bach, she described the experience.

> Yes, camping is wonderful—as always! Seriously, camping with these girls who come from the crowded New York tenements is a new experience for me in lots of ways. They seem to have the attitude of "me first and to heck with everyone else." It's a strange sensation—trying to explain a principle which you have always accepted without question—to a ten-year-old child. I'm really getting a great deal of valuable experience from this summer—broadening, if you know what I mean. I'll probably go around calling everyone "girlie" for at least the fall semester at school—but, it's worth it?!

> Letter, excerpt
> August, 1955

After Wally's graduation, Penny decided to leave school to marry him. They were married on August 3, 1956, at the First Presbyterian Church of Deerfield, Illinois. Witnessing all of the upscale ceremony of a regal fairy tale, guests later attended a reception at the fashionable Exmore Country Club in Highland Park. Judy Brunkow Glasford was Maid of Honor and bridesmaids were Joan Brunkow Ainsley and Karen Biddle Davis. Karen said that Penny was "deliberate, proud, confident, and fun-loving, although not particularly savvy."

This was an enchanting time of life for Penny. She had received many accolades for her academic and artistic achievements in high school and college, and had lived, and then married, in a setting of privilege. Like a sprightly blossom, Penny was pleased with how her life had unfolded and elated about the future. Questions were close at hand: ones that spoke boldly to her; others that only whispered.

Penny and Wally moved to Fort Monmouth, New Jersey, in the fall of 1956. Wally served a two-year commitment in the United States Army Signal Corp, an organization that managed communication and information systems to support the combined armed forces. This period was an adjustment for Penny, one in which she often felt lonely. Wally recalled that they befriended other officers and their wives which brightened Penny's days.

In 1958, they moved to Philadelphia, and Wally enrolled in the Wharton Graduate School of Business. As most newly married couples of that era, they were challenged to cover their living expenses. The economy of the times worked in their favor. A shortage of teachers enabled Penny to be hired by a New Jersey elementary school even though she did not yet have her education degree. Once again, she boldly lived her questions. Yet even greater courage and confidence would be needed in her immediate future.

In November of that year, Penny collapsed during an afternoon while teaching. School personnel surmised that Penny's blackout was due to pregnancy since other young, married female teachers had experienced similar symptoms. However, when Penny failed to respond to revival efforts, she was transported to a local hospital where tests diagnosed her with a cerebral aneurysm. Surgery was necessary.

Fortunately, her serious condition stabilized, giving Penny's mother time to fly from Chicago. Helen joined Wally at the hospital for a conversation with the staff surgeon. He recommended Dr. Van den Noordt, a prominent neurosurgeon in the area, to lead the effort. Penny was transferred to Bryn Mawr Hospital, and her surgery began in the early morning hours of the next day. Wally described the procedure as an eternity.

Penny was very lucky to have survived the surgery. She often told the story of how her skilled neurosurgeon was guided by his intuition to go against standard surgical protocol. Wally paraphrased Dr. Van den Noordt's words after the surgery. "He had to make a decision on which side of the brain to enter to perform the operation. If he had gone in on the wrong side, Penny would have died on the table." Additionally, the operation carried with it the risk of significant brain damage, potentially compromising her ability to read, write, sing or play piano.

During Penny's hospital recovery, Helen used hands-on healing to augment recuperation. Beginning at Penny's feet, Helen floated her hands upward over Penny's body, emitting healing energy. By the time Helen reached Penny's head, Penny opened her eyes, triggering a host of emotions for Helen.

This was the beginning of an extensive, two-year recovery effort, fueled by Penny's determination and Wally's assistance with memory flash cards. Penny healed, yet suffered some loss in the ability to read, write, and play piano. She also lost much of the field of vision in her right eye.[1]

Those close to Penny saw how these changes affected her. "Before the surgery," Wally recalled, "Penny was bubbly and very confident in her abilities. The aneurysm reduced her energy level and shook her confidence." Jan Bach, who maintained written communication, said that her handwriting changed, and that she became more reflective and thoughtful.

In the fall of 1960, Wally signed a contract with a consulting firm, and the couple moved to New York City. As the holidays approached, Penny became more introspective. She once again turned to writing. Her life over the next forty years would be mirrored by journal entries and poetry. However, long before she found the words, her heart understood.

> It is evening of the first serious snow of the season and I think of this small story [that is] partly about snow and partly about something else which is a mystery. It begins in Manhattan... years ago...
>
> I know no one in the city. I am also becoming painfully aware that my husband and I are poorly matched. There is nothing clear here.
>
> ...It snows all day. It announced on the radio that the city offices are closed as well as the

schools and everything else. When I look out, nothing is moving. I see one bundled, sexless pedestrian walking in the middle of the street, but that's all. Manhattan is completely still except for the sound of wind.

At six, my husband and I bundle up and walk the three flights of stairs to the street. We walk out into the night. No cabs, of course. We start walking the 15 blocks to our friends' apartment. It's not cold and the snow has stopped. Everything is covered with white and a nearly full moon makes the snow look eerie and beautiful.

I start to sing. It is an old folk song, familiar since childhood. Then, from the distance, I hear another voice singing this same song. It is a high and sweet voice, a few blocks ahead. I can barely make out the form of a boy, walking toward us. As he moves closer, I see his long, black coat and that he carries a violin case. We meet and stand together in the snow, singing. Then he smiles and walks on.

There is something about a mystery that draws us to it, not in order to understand but, for a moment, to live closely together. Every year with the first serious snow, I think of the boy in the long black coat, carrying a violin case, singing his way through the snow toward me.

"Snow," excerpts
December 4, 1996

Wally graduated from Wharton and accepted a position with the firm of Booz Allen Hamilton, a provider of management and technology services. He and Penny moved to Chicago.

Living so close to her mother must have been difficult for Penny. Helen

There is something about a mystery that draws us to it...

was often critical of Penny's dress and behavior. Chicago was Helen's home territory and a socially upscale territory at that. Helen prided herself on her status within the community and had expectations of Penny to conform. Equally strong, Penny was her own person with no intentions of compliance. To her, the move was an opportunity to demonstrate unspoken determination.

Continuing to listen to the bold voices within, Penny wanted to adopt a child. The couple contacted The Cradle, a well-known adoption agency in Evanston, Illinois. Karen came into their lives in June of 1962.

Who is this stranger
come from another woman's body,
placed in my arms, kicking
and staring blue-eyed up at me?

She is so like my first kitten
I held gingerly,
wrapped in newspaper, as we
drove home in the family car.

I am 22, holding
this blanketed bundle.
Foolishly, I think I know,
foolishly I believe she will
be like me.
As it turned out, only
a little of that was true.

And who is this woman,
blue-eyed, looking down at me?
Who is the woman who
still holds the kitten and the child,
not gingerly,
in the mystery of a daughter
now 30 years old?

"My Daughter's Birthday"
April 2, 1996

In October of 1963, Wally accepted a position with General Mills, and the Faster family of three moved to Minnesota. Penny was twenty-eight, and 4000 Hillcrest Road was a dream fulfilled. A large, two-storied white colonial, the house was surrounded on three sides by woods. The secluded property was a peaceful nature haven and perfect for Penny. Within two years of moving to Minnesota, Penny and Wally again approached The Cradle, this time adopting a son, Thomas.

> ...We adopted Tom when he was eight weeks old. Now he's 31. He's never been left behind when we've moved, but I'm not sure he knows that. Tom left for a football game when he was 16...Now he's back, has a dog, two cats, a wife, a computer and this business of trying to get stray animals adopted through the internet.
>
> ...*You have a dog, Casey,* said Tom. *I'll read her internet description: Black lab mix, six-years-old. Gentle and playful, good with children. Her picture is on the screen.*
>
> ...*I wonder if my new dog is like Casey, the famous baseball player?* I smiled contentedly.
>
> "Casey," excerpts
> July 21, 1998

Feeling comfortable and at ease in what would become long-term surroundings, Penny began to familiarize herself with her new community. The couple believed in the importance of forming a solid foundation for their new Minnesota life. They soon joined St. Luke Presbyterian Church, a relatively new congregation less than a mile from their home. St. Luke was then, and remains today, a unique Presbyterian church where members are "guided more by its commitment to peace, justice, and healing than by doctrines and dogmas."[2] At the time, Robert Hudnut, affectionately known as "Hud," was the minister.

Penny served a three-year term as an elder on the Session, the ruling body of St. Luke. Elder Lynn Cox was impressed that Penny seemed to make time for people, especially for the ones who struggled. She remembered Penny's gentle spirit, smile and talent for dance. Penny loved modern dance and occasionally performed individual liturgical dances. During other church services, Diane Williams and Deborah Cheney were also part of the dance performances.

> I am preparing a dance
> > with a woman I like.
> She is small and blonde.
> I am small with dark hair.
> > We are beginning
> > to make a dance together,
> > > instead of two solos danced simultaneously.
> I don't know how this happens.
> Is it the nature of the
> language of space?
> Space wants to speak and will.

> To make a dance is hard
> and easy, like breathing.
> What I love about dancing and breathing
> is the way my feet feel on the cool floor
> and how the air slides through
> my fingers.
> I love how my spirit wants to dance.

> I have always danced.
> As a child, I wanted
> > to be a bird.
> I jumped off the garage roof,
> > believing I could fly.
> > > I thought the same thing
> > > when I married at 20.

> After that I did not dance
> > for a long time
> > but that's not really true
> > as there were children

and I learned new dances
which were complicated
and simple.

Now I dance with my blonde friend
and I know I am afraid now
to dance, but I dance anyway.
My friend and I jump
off the garage roof.
We land lightly
on the earth.

"I Have Always Danced"
April 16, 1996

The church's mission was "Study, Share, Serve." Taking this to heart, Penny visited prison inmates and worked in a variety of ways to make the world a better place. She also joined a newly-formed sharing group, comprised of three to six couples, who met monthly in homes to share their life journeys, as well as an occasional dinner. Many deep and lasting adult relationships resulted, strengthening the fabric of the church and that of the general community.

The 1970s exposed unrest and social upheaval, brought on by the Vietnam War. Older generations were shocked by the brazen ideas and actions of younger generations. Venues for open discussion on previously taboo topics became increasingly important.

Bob Hudnut recalled that an idea for a new kind of sharing group resulted from a discussion with Penny. The group was to be cross-generational. Four adults and four teen members of the congregation would be recruited to participate. Ground rules stated that any subject was allowed for discussion. While members were expected to be respectful and affirming, complete openness and honesty were encouraged. "Hud" was profoundly moved as he observed passionate dialogues and honest, deep connections between members, unequaled in previous group experiences. He said that the group was transformative, and its success became a permanent part of his speaking repertoire.

One high school teen member of the group, Deborah Cheney, already knew Penny through a shared love of dance and empathy for the loss of Deborah's mother from an auto accident. Drawn to Penny's grace, poise, and natural beauty, Deborah also enjoyed Penny's wry humor. Penny projected a source of strength that made Deborah feel safe. She described Penny's behavior in the group as that of the "quintessential adult." Sharing within the new group led to a closer friendship between the women.

Over the months, Deborah sensed from discussions that Penny felt some discontent in her marriage, although she did not articulate that. Deborah believed that Penny and her husband were pursuing different goals. Jo Simonton Bolte, a new friend from the neighborhood and choir, also noted this same dissatisfaction in Penny. Fifteen years of living closely carried inherent mysteries of misunderstanding, transparent, yet impassable barriers.

In August 1971, Penny asked for a divorce. Devastating to Wally and the children, the separation was also upsetting to Helen who was very fond of Wally. No one knows exactly why Penny chose that particular time to make a drastic change in her life. One can only speculate.

A number of factors made divorce more compelling and also more acceptable. Penny certainly did not have a relationship with another man; that was not her style. At thirty-six, she knew that she was highly resourceful, and that Wally's business success would translate to an adequate financial outcome. Early in her marriage, Penny realized that she and Wally were not a good fit. Her personality was carefree, creative, and desired emotional connection. His was practical, deliberate, and self-sustaining.

Additionally, divorce no longer carried the stigma that society had once imposed and was embraced by the St. Luke culture. Penny would find support there. Yet her decision may have been less calculating. Perhaps she simply was not able to endure the lack of connection in the relationship. True to herself, she chose to cope with the consequences of her decision, to rely on her resourcefulness, and to move on with her life as an unemployed, single mom.

You do not have to be good.
You do not have to walk on your knees
for a hundred miles through the desert, repenting.
You only have to let the soft animal of your body
    love what it loves.
Tell me about despair, yours, and I will tell you mine.
Meanwhile the world goes on.
Meanwhile the sun and the clear pebbles of the rain
are moving across the landscapes,
over the prairies and the deep trees,
the mountains and the rivers.
Meanwhile the wild geese, high in the clear blue air,
are heading home again.
Whoever you are, no matter how lonely,
the world offers itself to your imagination,
calls to you like the wild geese, harsh and exciting—
over and over, announcing your place
in the family of things.

"*Wild Geese*"[3]
Mary Oliver

...to move on

I walk beside the lake at dawn.
The air is warm for October close to
        Lake Superior.
The lake holds its light close to
        its body like a child with insufficient clothing.

I walk slowly over the grey rocks
        watching the water, the grey sky.
In the brush ahead, there is a sound.
A person? An animal? The vibratory
        sound of pain?
My breath is short. There is a
        whirring in my chest.

In the brush ahead, barely hidden,
        A full-grown black bear.
He is about my height.
He sits facing me, leaning heavily on
        the trunk of a small tree.

His eyes are closed.
The flesh of his left arm is torn to
        the tendon.
It is bleeding , the pink
        of the beginning dawn.

I am strangely not afraid.
I am as helpless as he is.
There is no philosophy that can
        help us, no act.

He makes the sound again and
        opens his eyes.
His body is completely still.
In his throat, he sounds his pain.

The light comes pink and light blue
        over the water.

I sit down on the rocks and
wait with him.

Journal entry
October 17, 1995

Chapter 6
Thin Places

After her divorce, Penny chose a life of substance over a life of privilege. For the next six years she studied and worked long hours, building a foundation for a self-directed and sustainable new life. She enrolled in the University of Minnesota and completed her education undergraduate degree with high distinction in the area of Therapeutic Recreation. Two years later, in 1977, she graduated from the same university, earning a Master of Arts in Communication Theory.

Her commute to the University of Minnesota by freeway took about thirty minutes; however, Pen was uncomfortable driving on the freeways because of her compromised eyesight. Instead, she chose to use city streets, nearly doubling her driving time. She also tried to avoid heavy traffic by leaving early in the morning which gave her time to study before class. A challenging routine, no doubt this period of her life was frustrating, stressful, and scary. Wanting to compensate for these feelings and to control some part of her life, she most likely became tight with boundaries and tight with money. As a result, her children, Karen and Tom, probably felt the effects of her constriction.

If I pay little attention, everything looks the same in the woods.

The early morning sun slants across the green grass and into the trees on the west. In the Native American tradition, west is the direction of inner knowing. Though I sense a foothold in the west, the rest of my body waves in the wind. My old companion, fear, is ever present. As I look again at the slant of the sun, I realize that the sun's light is coming from the east.

Eastern directionality relates to "our greatest spiritual challenges." What are mine? Blending opposites: being more deeply inward and more clearly outward, giving and receiving, witnessing and acting, even loving and hating, beauty and ugliness, surprise and control, anticipating and remembering.

I have asked in prayer to see fully both with my two eyes and my heart. I am learning how painful it is to have this prayer answered.

Journal entry
September 10, 1996

When Penny wanted to escape from the demands of life, she chose the companionship of nature; it helped her to reconnect with her inner truth. Accepting her exactly as she was in the moment, without asking questions, the natural world let her simply exist.

> Listen.
>> Snow's voice
>> is the sound of wings
>> and in this field
>> the animals
>> shake their shaggy heads
>> speak the sounds they know.
> Even sweet stars sing.
> And something in me opens--
>> something large like love or prayer
>> or silence--
>> something I carry in my arms
>> like a child.

Christmas Collection
2001

Even sweet stars sing

I finally "got religion,"
but not like the shiny-faced
and smiling people on
the TV gospel shows.

From the kitchen window
I watch the rain
come down,
warm and silver,
on the grass.

By 11, the sun shines
and lopes across the
wet grass like a puppy.
Whatever religion
is, it is as
feathered and strong and
light as the
small birds now gathering
on the wet
grass to drink.

"Getting Religion"
June 7, 2001

Religion and spirituality posed unending questions, and Penny spent many hours in seminars and in spiritual self-study. Determined to get professional input, she joined discussions with a number of pastors. Additionally, she studied scholarly commentary.

Her continuing quest to live her questions was, in part, satisfied by the work of Paul Tillich, a theologian who explored what it meant to be a finite human being, and by that of Stephen Patterson of Eden Theological Seminary in St. Louis. Penny became acquainted with his book, THE GOD OF JESUS: THE HISTORICAL JESUS AND THE SEARCH FOR MEANING, through a morning study group led by Reverend Newby. Professor Patterson offered passages that made sense to her — a simple model of what Jesus believed about God: "To love one's neighbor *is* to love God. For to love God is to love love itself. That is why Jesus embodied love in his own life in a more radical way than the simple love of neighbor might suggest…He loved sinners, traitors, tax collectors…He loved his enemies."[1] Penny understood neighbor as an umbrella term that referred to creations of the universe, particularly those that were vulnerable, including animals. According to Reverend Newby, "Penny knew this understanding of love…this reality that can give life its richness and meaning."[2] Penny loved with all of her being. Nothing about her love was superficial.

Another biblical scholar whose work Penny valued was Marcus J. Borg, author of THE HEART OF CHRISTIANITY. His writing spoke of the heart as a metaphor for the inner self—deeper than perception, intellect, emotion or will. When the heart is most open, the veil of the afterlife lifts for a short time, allowing the experience of feeling God. This is described as a "thin place"—where the boundary between self and world becomes one, or as Borg explained, "anywhere our hearts are opened."[3] Penny most often experienced "thin places" in nature; however, as Borg cited, "…music, poetry, literature, the visual arts and dance can all become thin places…"[4]

> Somehow you got in—
> a waft of wind,
> an open door.
> There'll be a fuss
> when the janitor comes.
>
> …Well, I'm glad for your company,
> the witness of your black eye.
> I move the chairs,
> clear a circle of space.
>
> Clear a circle in my head
> For the muse of my body—…
>
> Crow is still—
> watches
> as I do him
> then I turn, slowly at first.

Now fast,
  take up legions
  of space —
"There must be some mistake," he says,
"or is this some poor-ass way of flying?"

Well, I say to him,
  "Crow, if I were rich,
  I'd buy crows for all
  the churches and there'd
  be no questions
  asked, none
  answered."

"Crow and Dancer in Church," excerpts
August 13, 2001

When living the questions of life, progress in understanding spirituality and where one is on its path can be difficult to gauge. Sometimes unknowns are best explained in terms of things familiar. Penny persevered.

Is it bigger than a bread box,
  longer than the wide woods
  behind the house?
Is it as small as a moment
  or the tiny, dark turds left by
  a mouse who has taken up
  residence in our warm house.
When I look out into the woods,
  can I see it in the bare trees,
  in the rain, the grey sky,
  in the flashing red cardinal
  on the feeder?
Can I hear it in music?
When I cut up a pickle
  and eat it, and the juice
  gets all over my mouth,
  is this spiritual?

71

It is raining hard now,
    cold and hard.
Only one squirrel has run across
    the grass of our lawn all
    morning.
Can I assume the rest
    are somewhere warm in
    the nests they build in our
    monumental piles of brush
    and leaves a distance from
    the house?
What is longer and wider and
    higher than the wide woods
    behind the house?

"Questions about Spirituality"
October 22, 1996

In her undergraduate and graduate work, Penny had studied the advent of dance therapy pioneered in the 1930s by Marian Chace.[5] This new venue for psychotherapy provided another platform for addressing social, emotional and physical challenges. It focused on body language, rather than on verbal skills, and was successfully used in psychiatric and rehabilitation facilities, schools, nursing homes, drug treatment centers, and counseling centers.[6]

Personal experience confirmed another thin place in Penny's life. A dancer, she felt stress leave her as she moved in response to the connection with her higher self. With this anecdotal evidence, she determined to work in dance therapy where she could help others more effectively manage their emotions.

The movement therapy program at Abbott Northwestern Hospital in Minneapolis appealed to Penny, and she interviewed for a therapist position. In June 1978, she was hired as a mental health therapist and eagerly started her new career.

Penny's mentor at Abbott Northwestern was Dr. Alice Bovard-Taylor who said that Penny learned quickly. Bovard-Taylor, a pioneer and charter member of the American Dance Therapy Association, developed psychology-based dance therapy programs at several Minneapolis hospitals.

Leslie Wittels Marble, a program colleague who first met Penny in 1979, stated, "Penny took wonderful care of herself, both physically and spiritually. She was authentic to a tee, saying 'yes' when she meant yes and 'no' when she meant no. Penny was funny, loving, a caring friend, and gracious. She didn't apologize for who she was or how she did things. And, in being so much herself, she was so perfectly whole and worthy of absolute acceptance."

A good friend and movement therapist at Abbott, Marylee Hardenbergh, recalled peer supervision discussions with Penny and Leslie about meeting times. Early morning meetings were difficult for Marylee to attend, and Penny declined to meet after work because she reserved those hours for personal meditation. Although Marylee had hoped for a different outcome, the colleagues agreed to meet during the early hours of the day. Marylee said that she respected Penny's ability to keep her boundaries.

Kate Gardos Reid joined the Abbott group in January of 1987. She reminisced that Penny was a lively, professional colleague who absolutely loved her work and laughed often at jokes. Penny's team members said that she developed her own interventions, especially with borderline personality patients, and enjoyed sharing her discoveries at meetings. I was fortunate to learn about the impact of Penny's work from one of her private clients.

> "My husband and I were referred to Penny by Marylee Hardenbergh who said, 'If you want to do movement therapy, Penny is the best person to go to.'
>
> Penny had impeccable boundaries which created a safe therapy environment. Intensely creative as a practitioner, both in terms of theoretical and practical interventions, she could create and design an intervention on-the-spot. An example was a movement exercise

in which she asked us to support each other physically. This helped us to better understand the support we weren't getting.

Penny was highly knowledgeable in childhood development, specifically incorporating the theories of Judith Kestenberg.[7] Penny was brilliant in creating movement exercises that helped me to fill in my developmental gaps. She was one of the most effective helpers I have known."

Client telephone interview
May 20, 2012

My first job
was dancing with autistic children,
one by one.

We would spin,
hands with hands,
across the floor

and I would knock
at the door of themselves.
Sometimes it opened a wedge through their eyes.

And I said,
time is a ribbon.
Long ribbons and
short are equally beautiful.

What did the child see
through that wedge of time?
Was it a spark?
Was it a voice, calling?

Christmas Collection
2004

Snow is spiraling down in
        no hurry unlike February
        snow, eager to lash and whip.
The latch on the barn door
        is heavy, the light dim.
I come into the world of
        cats and chickens underfoot,
        walk carefully to where
        the ewe stands, solemn
        and luminous,
        her two new lambs beside
        her on legs shaky as an
        old table's.
The lambs flick their ears,
        stare at me as if trying
        to remember something, perhaps
        the warm womb.
I reach my hand to the
        ewe. She shakes her head
and paws the straw. I crouch down and wait as
may be necessary in the beginning
        of any friendship.
But the smaller of the two
lambs, the black one, moves toward me on
wobbly legs, bypasses my out-stretched
        hand, presses her small
        mouth on my cheek.
I'm not sure what has
        been born in her, but I can
        tell you her mouth was cool
        and her body smelled sweet
        like the straw and that I
        believe all friendship is
        a mystery.
I walked out into the April snow
        which also seemed to welcome
        me in its own way.

Slender black lamb says,
"Remember—more things move
than blood to the heart."

"April and the Lambs"
March, 1998

Chapter 7
Push and Pull

I had been thrust into the experiment, and it was all very scary and upsetting. After the tragedy of her brother's suicide, my wife at the time told me that she was re-evaluating our marriage. I was shocked to hear her words. She and two other female friends, also discontented with their marriages, decided that the collective husbands should move out and rent an apartment together for one month. After that time, the husbands would return to their homes, and the women would rent an apartment together. I felt as if I were being sucked into the eye of a storm with no way out. Believing strongly in the integrity of the family unit, I found this plan very troubling.

When I met with friends, our conversations danced around the elephant in the room. No one would listen, and that's all I really wanted. Frustrated, I looked for help in another direction—the St. Luke Presbyterian Church Community. Although a newcomer to the congregation, I decided to take action. My plan was to meet individually over lunch with four female acquaintances; one was the minister at the time and another was Penny. Even though I barely knew her, she seemed approachable.

We decided to meet at the Walker Art Center cafeteria. With its bright, cheerful ambiance, it also featured good food. It was March of 1982. I met Penny inside the main entrance to the "Walker" as it was known, coincidentally Penny's maiden name. Pen was highly attractive in a white jacket with a fur collar. I did not even guess that it was faux fur; later I would learn that Pen never would have worn real fur. I remembered her shyness, her genuineness, and her smile. What I didn't know was that Penny, a single mom for nine years, already had identified me as a person of interest should the circumstances be right.

In a few brief moments, my anxiety vanished. Penny's avid listening style boosted my confidence. A brief summary of my situation naturally emerged. Penny listened with sweetness and kindness. How, out of the blue, my wife was reassessing our marriage with two, wonderful children. How I thought our union was impeccably solid. How I was absolutely stunned. She continued to listen, and that is what I will always remember.

Suddenly, I felt a glimmer of hope in my dismal situation. Looking back, it was the beginning of a journey of growth; of transformation and bonding; and ultimately, of challenge, loss and healing.

> Very still.
> Stars bright.
> Clear, December night.
> Cold comes in, even through our padded gloves.
>
> We stand in a clearing
> a distance from the house
> bringing in wood for the fire,
> piling logs into the wheelbarrow.
> We push our load up the hill —
> Hard work and joyful —
> For how else can we know the closeness
> of the stars and the stillness?
> How else can we know the intimate
> welcome of this night of promise?
>
> *Christmas Collection*
> 1993

After our initial luncheon meeting, I felt strength from being with Penny and was drawn to her friendship. I still worked full time, spent time with my children, and participated in the daily chores of living. Separation from my wife continued after the experiment. Penny trusted her intuition, and it told her that we were meant to be together. She told me once that she asked her spirit guides for direction and was given an image of a lioness patiently waiting. With that in mind, she decided to take me in and wait until I came to understand the gem that she was. Only then would she know the depth of love that she had wanted for so long.

I continued to be highly upset and self-centered, not the kind of mindset that led to an appreciation of the positive qualities of a woman of such depth. I was not ready for, nor was I interested in, a romantic relationship. Not only was Penny willing to hold a space of recovery for me as I coped with my loss, but she actually found herself falling in love with me. I was oblivious. In retrospect, I don't know how I got so lucky. It was like winning the lottery.

While I was not in love with Penny, nor able to be in love with anyone under the circumstances, I did realize that she and I shared similarities. We both loved to be in nature and felt strongly about protecting it. Both of us also connected with God through nature. Introverts, both of us were also enthusiastic runners. We enjoyed subtle senses of humor and laughed at the same things. I started paying closer attention to these prophetic, almost harmonic convergences.

> ... The Buddhists say
> > the only reality is impermanence,
> > but I don't think I
> > believe that.
> There is something so permanent
> > about singing.

"Singing on a Cold and Clear Day," excerpt
November 15, 1996

Then the other side of the coin surfaced. Both of us needed financial strength to feel safe. Penny was anxious about relationships. Male abandonment had been a major issue for her, and she feared my breaking off our relationship. The crux for me: Was I spending so much time with Penny that my children were feeling abandoned? I also lacked confidence about my physical health. We each had concerns and were challenged to deeper reflections.

Unknown to me, yet unearthed in her diary entries years later, was the vulnerability she felt in opening her heart to me. A single entry of March 16, 1982, revealed her deepest feelings: "Two summers ago, I let myself feel the emptiness that had been there all of my life."

...the only reality is impermanence

So much has happened in a month that has exposed me, deepened me. I want to simply experience who I am becoming—without fear or attempt to control. I want to make room for who I am becoming.

Being so connected to another person feels really new for me—pretty scary. I sometimes do weird things around scaredness [sic]—sometimes I pull away to be less vulnerable. I hope he will put up with all this. He is so dear. I love him so much I refuse to be run around by my scaredness [sic].

In my more honest moments, I allow myself to feel how important you are to me—this is frightening to me tonight. I think I want to be braver—to know that loving is a very difficult business, to know it takes a lifetime, to know that my loving is not dependent on another's response. The strange mixture stays with me—happiness and fear. Maybe I am not so brave. I didn't know loving you would require me to work so hard.

Diary entry
April 12, 1982

During this period of our courtship, Penny went to work two hours early one day, arriving before 5 A.M. to use the recording equipment there to create a custom audio tape for me. She selected a variety of songs that she knew I'd like from the 1960s by vocalists such as Joan Baez and Judy Collins and groups like Peter Paul and Mary. Pachelbel's "Canon in D" was also included.

I loved Penny's fun and silliness. True to her younger days, she composed this limerick after a week's trip to Sarasota, Florida, to visit Helen and her second husband, George Stanwood.

At last! The day to fly back home.
Over the land, over the foam.
Whoopie and splatters.
What really matters?

A hug from David and love I show 'm.

P.S. This is a homecoming limerick.

Journal entry
April 15, 1985

The highlight of the first four months of our relationship was our trip to
the North Shore of Lake Superior. We stayed near Tofte in a cabin with a
deck that overlooked the lake. Penny grew to love the North Shore for its
natural beauty and for the mystery of Lake Superior—a huge, glistening
body of cold water, the largest fresh water lake in the world. It was on this
trip that I first made Penny roll with laughter. She said something that
reminded me of the old adage: "Never teach a pig to sing. It's a waste of
your time, and it annoys the pig." Penny howled. She wrote the verse in
her journal, entering it under "Matters of Consequence."

A constant companion, her journal was forthcoming with comments about
this trip:

1. Gin Rummy: Bos is a lousy loser.
2. Cribbage: Pretty dumb game. The definition of a
   dumb game is one I don't know how to play.
3. Carlton Peak: Hard work getting there; we find
   a place on the rocks where we can see for miles.
   Incredibly beautiful. Endless green trees and
   beyond, endless blue water of Lake Superior,
   then endless sky. An arrow points to a steep
   path. We find footholds up the path of rock.
   The highest point we see [in] all directions.
   The beginning of the Sawbill Trail points toward
   home. An ore boat is moving out into the lake.
4. We agree that everything makes sense if seen
   from enough distance.
5. I learn: I like people more than I thought. I like
   you more than I thought. You are quiet. I am not
   sure of what you are learning. You love the
   North Shore, feel as though you are coming
   home to have time with a beloved friend.

"North Shore"
June 19-21, 1982

As the summer rolled on with school still in recess, it became more and more difficult for me to balance my relationship with my family and time with Pen. She realized that I was struggling and wondered what I thought about continuing our relationship. We decided to take a break. I was relieved because I could focus on my children.

A few months later, Penny called me, and we reunited. In the fall of 1984, I sold my home and moved in with Penny. I rented a U-Haul truck, and my friend, Bob "Ace" Merrill, helped me move my meager possessions, including a large couch and a chest of drawers, to 4000 Hillcrest Road, Deephaven. An old snowblower accompanied me, a tool that would come in handy to clear the unusually long driveway of her home. Penny was very excited and had worked hard to make me feel at home. Our new life together began, a highly significant chapter for each of us.

Relationships are complex and, even with the best of intentions, can be challenging. Although my career positioned me as the head of an investment advisory arm of a regional financial services firm, Swenson Anderson Associates, my monies were already divided between monthly spousal maintenance and child support. At that point I represented minimal financial strength to Penny.

Additionally, I was still grieving the loss of my immediate family and all of its complexities. My children, Meg and Chris, wanted to live in one home, rather than move between two residences. They ultimately decided to live with my former wife. This news came after Penny and I had spent considerable time and resources renovating rooms for them in her home. Penny's children, Karen and Tom, no longer lived there.

Penny felt a strong need for closure and quick resolution of most unresolved issues. I, on the other hand, deferred major decisions, hoping that either time would resolve them or the answer would become clear or less important. Pen often thought I was too slow in dealing with an issue. She kidded me that I had two speeds—slow and slower. Yet, the process worked for my temperament and often worked to our mutual advantage. I thought of the process as "positioning myself" and would kid Pen by saying, "Penroe, you've got to position yourself." That always made Penny laugh, and it was astonishing how often the process proved beneficial.

It was only a matter of time before I opened my heart to new possibilities. Setting a wedding date of October 12, 1985, we chose the garden court of St. Luke Presbyterian Church as the setting for our small wedding. We invited family and close friends to a ceremony that reflected our values of simplicity, frugality, environmental consciousness, and a lifelong commitment to each other. Later, guests gathered for a reception in our home on that clear day, amid a stunning blaze of fall color. It seemed like the perfect omen for our life together as committed partners.

While I felt underqualified to be the partner of a woman with such strength and depth, I grew into the job under her tutelage. Penny and I were nearly a perfect match and shared a very compassionate and gentle spirit to the depths of our being.

> I love you with the part of me that is quiet,
> watching the wind move the trees.
> I love you with the part of me that runs in the
> warm rain, watching a pair of cardinals in the
> branches of a bare tree — that listens and loves
> their song.
>
> I love you with the part of me that misses you
> tonight that remembers your warm body, your
> gentle touch.
> I love you with the part of me that is afraid.
> I love you with the part of me that first allowed,
> then welcomed you into the deepest parts of me
> that I did not know or understand.
>
> And you touch all these parts of me gently, with
> great care as one holding a sleeping animal in
> his arms.
>
> Journal entry
> March 29, 1982

"I've learned this much about marriage…
You get tested. You find out who you are,
who the other person is, and how you
accommodate or don't. …

"Still," he said, "there are a few rules I
know to be true about love and marriage:
If you don't respect the other person,
you're gonna have a lot of trouble. If you
don't know how to compromise, you're
gonna have a lot of trouble. If you can't talk
openly about what goes on between you,
you're gonna have a lot of trouble. And
if you don't have a common set of values
in life, you're gonna have a lot of trouble.
Your values must be alike.

And the biggest one of those values,
Mitch?"

"Yes?"

"Your belief in the *importance* of your
marriage."

TUESDAYS WITH MORRIE[1]
Mitch Albom

Chapter 8
Rhythms in Time

Penny and I harmonized perfectly with Morrie Schwartz's marriage
criteria. We were interested in many of the same things. We respected
each other and the vows we had made to one another. Each of us believed
in honoring commitments. As we explored nature, participated in our
church community, built investments, and pursued our interests in music
and the arts, we continued to grow closer and closer. I gradually fell in love
with Penny and, as that love deepened, our bond became more resilient.

I believed another component of a successful marriage was defining my share or contribution and then freely offering it to all aspects of our union. For a number of years, I thought and hoped that I was contributing more to the relationship than Penny was. Only later did I discover that I was mistaken—a share did not keep track; it was spontaneous and heartfelt.

On a Friday in the fall of 1989, I was at work when I began to feel extremely anxious. I had promised Penny that I would buy a pair of cross country skis for her at Hoigaard's, a St. Louis Park store specializing in outdoor gear and apparel. As the afternoon continued, I felt so lightheaded from anxiety that the mere act of making this purchase became an ordeal. I managed to buy the skis, but I couldn't dismiss the thought of my rising adrenaline. Once home, I was afraid that I would never be able to stop the mounting anxiety. I had experienced abnormal anxiety before, yet nothing to this extent.

Penny was not a caretaker personality; however, she was concerned and tried to help me. She worked with a number of psychiatrists at the hospital where she was employed and felt that Dr. James Guerrero did excellent work. She called him late that same afternoon, and I became his patient. What followed were weeks and months of living terror, fearing not being able to function at a level required for my job. I'm still unable to account for how I survived that time at work; I just did the best I could and gave silent thanks as each day closed. Then it was on to another night with minimal sleep. This debilitation waxed and waned over a period of several years. During that time, Penny often encouraged me to remember that I had power over my anxiety, that it was not a major concern, and that I would defeat it. I desperately wanted Dr. Guerrero to tell me that I would recover from performance anxiety. He did not, and that made me angry. In retrospect, this was a gift to me, one that left me no other choice but to work through my torment. Over time, I became stronger.

A fearful side to our personalities, Penny and I learned to counteract anxiety to feel more comfortable. After reading all of Penny's journals and learning about her life before I knew her, I think we both shared a strong need to achieve. One way she learned to cope with her performance anxiety was to prepare far in advance. For example, if she had an appointment at an unfamiliar location, she would ask me to drive her there a day or two beforehand. If there was a task confronting her, she would immediately embrace it to allow enough time for completion.

Another example of Penny's extended preparation was writing her annual Christmas poem sometimes nine or ten months prior to the holiday season. Penny loved to write and, self-admittedly, could not keep from writing. Her journaling openly weighed a lingering affliction that is common to many writers.

> I am hopeful and curious about my writing. Do I dare to believe that I could be a writer—be an artist and philosopher in that way? Is that my place in the order of things? Is writing my contribution to the world? I am such a novice, so unsure of my ability, so fearful. But I do sense myself moving forward in some mysterious way, though the end result seems so obscure.

> Journal entry, excerpt
> August 13, 1996

> I see myself standing nose to nose
>   with my writer self.
> I am so well-defined in my jeans and
>   red sweatshirt.
> Muscles firm, flesh tight over my cheekbones.
> My other self is transparent,
>   almost unformed, naked, leaning
>   against the door
>   like a newborn animal who is
>   unsure of the length of its own
>   body.

> I know them both intimately,
>   Know that one cannot survive
>   without the other,
> Know how much I need them both.
> Know how much I hate to think
>   about them.
> Know they may be laughing at me.
> Know that's O.K.

Journal entry
December 4, 1995

I'm back to being scared about writing, that
I'm not good enough—the critic is driving my
bus. Where does that voice come from? I think,
Mother. I can hear her correcting my singing
as an adolescent and suggesting I change my
dress when I was about to attend my bridal
shower. How long the voices linger; how firmly
they are embedded in my belief system. It isn't
enough to understand. I believe the road home
to myself is to gently defy the message.

The woods help. They are so alive and so
beautiful, so   undefended and without
judgment. So I will be the witness for the woods.
Doesn't everyone want a legacy, someone or
something to reflect them?

So I shall write about ambitious squirrels who
push the corn cobs from the feeder all the way
across the snow tracks; the juncos and cardinals
at our feeder; the pair of enormous crows, black
against the snow; and most of all, the families
of deer that come to the feeder at twilight.

These   loved   creatures will be and are my
bridge to myself. I thank them daily in my
heart. I show them my appreciation by keeping
our ground level feeder tended during the dark
and cold months when food is scarce.

Journal entry
January 7, 1997

We both shared a love of running. One beautiful day, Penny and I decided
to run together at Lake of the Isles, a short distance from downtown
Minneapolis. I remember how excited and determined she was to keep

These loved creatures will be and are my bridge to myself...

Siesta Key Beach, Sarasota County, Florida

up with me, which she did. I was running a mile in under eight minutes and was impressed with Pen's competitiveness and physical endurance. She was, after all, seven years older than I. Neither a good movie nor sex — perhaps winning the lottery — could compare to a good, hard run outside on a gorgeous day.

During the late 1980s and early 1990s, Penny and I started to travel as part of our routine. Although homebodies at heart, especially Penny, we were attracted to the warm climates of relocations involving some of our closest relatives. Helen and George retired to Sarasota, Florida. My children, Meghan and Chris, remained in Arizona after their graduations from Northern Arizona University in Flagstaff.

When in Sarasota, Pen and I especially enjoyed Siesta Key Beach and Pelican Man's Bird Sanctuary. Still rated as the best beach in the country, Siesta Key Beach is known for its powdered sugar quartzite sand. We often walked the four-mile stretch of inviting softness and swam as well. The bird sanctuary had two missions. One was to educate the public about how wildlife could be better protected from their misadventures with humans and the other was to rescue, rehabilitate, and release injured birds. Long-standing respect for wildlife and its protection were deep values for both of us.

Reconnecting with college friends, Judy and Joan Brunkow, led to a trip to Santa Fe, New Mexico. We had heard positive comments about Santa Fe from others and wanted to visit Judy Brunkow Glasford and her husband, Jim. They invited us to see their work-in-progress retirement home, a bonus that we couldn't refuse. While there, we also toured the Georgia O'Keefe Museum of Art and drove to Ghost Ranch, a Presbyterian retreat center that was familiar to many St. Luke members.

Even though we preferred staying home to traveling, we found that leaving town was easier when we thought of our trips as segments. The first segment was anticipation and preparation for the trip. Next was the actual trip to reach our destination. The last segment was the return trip home. For Penny, the homecoming was the best part about taking trips to new places. I regarded the first segment as the best part of the trip.

I joked with Pen about how segmenting the parts of a trip epitomized the "tight shoe theory": It was almost worth wearing a too-tight shoe just for the pleasure of taking off the damn thing. For Pen, that theory also fit most types of outdoor adventures, especially camping trips and daily runs in rain or bitter cold. Running in adverse conditions gave her the double reward of feeling like a heroine for completing her goal and delighting in the joyous release of removing the "tight shoe." There is nothing quite like the liberation from uncomfortable deprivation. It's just the best.

Together, Pen and I discovered a number of nature havens. Carver Park, part of the Hennepin County Park System with thirty-six miles of nature trails, is just west of the Minneapolis metro area. Penny had a keen appreciation of the subtleties of prairie color and textures that many others did not see. Often our Saturday entertainment was to walk in Carver Park and then listen to *A Prairie Home Companion*,[2] a Minnesota Public Radio (MPR) program, with Garrison Keillor.

> ...Also this week, David and I had our 11th Anniversary. We celebrated by hiking at Carver [Park] in the late afternoon. It was good as Carver always is. A warm and sunny day for mid October, we walked the familiar back road trail. Trees muted in color, goldenrod had turned brown. We heard the call of an owl, footsteps from the woods of a large animal we could not see (probably a deer or a fox), and heard millions of crickets. The crickets made such a racket. Then we came home and had burgers and fresh tomatoes from our garden.
>
> I don't know what I think about our 11th Anniversary — sort of like asking a fish what he thinks about the water. But I know I love David with my whole heart.
>
> Journal entry, excerpt
> October 15, 1996

Perseverance challenged us during a trip to Hazelglade Resort on Mille Lacs Lake. My daughter, Meg, was with us. A resort guest reported that a kitten had been left stranded a mile from shore on Father Hennepin's Rock, a small island — some might describe it as a pile of rocks — with little vegetation. An abandoned animal struck a chord in our hearts.

Mille Lacs had a reputation as a large, relatively shallow lake that quickly could become treacherous. The surface was already choppy that day, and I doubted the safety of being on the water. However, Pen and Meg shared a passionate interest in protecting animals and were determined to rescue the kitten. Venturing out in a fishing boat, the southern winds at our backs, we were armed with only a towel, small dish, and a container of milk. The water became rougher and rougher as three-foot breakers targeted us. As if on a rollercoaster, we made our way toward the island. Nearly there, I throttled down for our approach. The motor died.

I reached out at some large, jutting rocks, dismissing thoughts of possible injuries. Finally securing our position, I stepped out onto solid ground. Not far away was the scared kitten that immediately lapped up my offering of milk. I picked up the kitten and handed it to Penny who wrapped the animal in the towel for the return trip.

Our safety was still in jeopardy. Tenseness escalated as I tried to restart the motor while Pen and Meg joined forces to hold the boat to the protected side of the rock pile. No luck! A long, arduous row in dangerous waves was not a welcomed option. All ears were on the motor. A string of expletives, followed by reluctant puttering, led to a fully-firing motor. After our safe return, we decided to name the kitten Mille Lou initially. Later, we switched it to Louis when we discovered its gender. Since Pen already had two cats, Meg agreed to take Louis home. He became a wonderful pet.

In our early years together, Penny was quite frugal. For Christmas one year, I gave her a new suitcase to replace the very worn and ragged one she had. Pen insisted that I return it! She kidded and talked about being a cheap date, but it was just who she was, and I think she was proud of it. Not spending excessively was an important value to her — something she just thought was wrong. I believed in that value also, but was a bit more flexible. Financial security was our goal, and unnecessary spending detracted from it.

Pen and I shared a passion for music, although her taste was much more sophisticated than mine. She preferred Mozart and Aaron Copland, while I liked to sing along with Arlo Guthrie and the Nashville Bluegrass Band. Pen definitely expressed some concern when I listened to a particularly hokey piece on a Bluegrass Saturday morning radio program. She would ask, "Now, do you *really* like that, Bro?" I would usually say, "No," which would offer her some reassurance that I was not totally beyond redemption.

Penny's step-grandmother, Georgia, quite adored her and left her an inheritance sufficient to purchase a Steinway baby grand piano. In spite of her aneurysm-induced surgery of earlier decades that created a loss of certain musical skills, Penny was able to sit at the keyboard and occasionally play from memory. The instrument was a source of endearing joy.

After we married, I chorded music as Penny sang along. I played every day after work. Soon Pen suggested that we join the St. Luke choir. Its repertoire covered country to classics, from Handel to Bob Marlow, and we loved singing every Sunday for over fifteen years. We also sang in the St. Luke Folk Choir.

The accompaniment for our selections often included a banjo, a bass, or a mandolin. Sometimes I played my guitar—not in a remarkably accomplished way—yet I was passionate. In front of a group, I had a tendency to be anxious with sweaty palms and temporarily arthritic fingers taking charge. For our first solo performance in front of the congregation, Penny and I chose "Swing Low, Sweet Chariot." We planned to sing a duet to my guitar accompaniment. Scheduled to perform at the beginning of the service as everyone was getting settled, we believed that our contribution would go largely unnoticed.

However, experience that morning taught me to expect the unexpected. A piano solo was scheduled prior to our performance and, as the ending chord sounded, the sanctuary became a vacuum. I struggled to control my anxiety. Everyone surely heard my heart beat. Pen's last words to me were, "Now Bro, remember, don't go too fast." We began. I started out slowly, but kept going faster and faster. We finished. Afterward, our choir director said, "I thought you guys were going to crash and burn!" Fortunately, St. Luke was a very forgiving place.

Our marriage provided similar nurturing. We honored the rhythm of our individual temperaments, yet understood the cadence of differences and practiced forgiveness. Our commitment to each other was first and foremost.

> ...It has been a good week—soft rhythms of time
> following each other in a moving circle.
> These rhythms have held the
> blessed ordinary events of my life:
> Physical work
> Rest
> Cooking and cleaning
> Meditating and silence
> Working with clients
> Watching the weather
> Time with David.
>
> I am learning slowly how precious,
> yes, sacred these things are.
> Help me to be awake to each
> nuance of these rhythms.
> Help me be slow enough to see it all
> from both the outside and the
> inside.
>
> Journal entry, excerpt
> March 12, 1996

So cold today — well below zero — the cold runs up my legs and bites my face, in fact, bites all the parts of my body except my trunk which is secured by layers of clothing and my old down jacket. My mother gave me the money for the now somewhat lumpy, maroon jacket almost twenty years ago — her contribution to my survival in Minnesota winters.

…Watching the birds and animals at our two feeders gives us such great pleasure…I am especially fond of the female cardinals. They are not aggressive like the large, grey squirrels who challenge any other creature at the feeder by running headlong at them.

…And none of the creatures complain, with the possible exception of the large, grey squirrels. They accept the cold and snow and live in the moment. They teach me to do the same.

Journal entry, excerpts
January 14, 1997

Chapter 9
Old Love

A "country of two," we often spoke of how lucky we were to share our love, the many amenities of our Minnesota location, and our routines. A large part of our relationship was learning to focus on the here and now, the current moment, without giving power to the past or yearning for the future. The love we shared gave us comfort beyond our years together, and we thrived on the simplicity, bliss, and ease of being with each other.

CHORUS: We've got an old love
One we never will get tired of
One that fits us like an old glove
One to warm a winter's day

We don't have to say I love you
Quite as often as we used to
Old love just goes without saying
But we still say it anyway.

VERSE: We may not leave this town we live in
Life's not as easy as we planned
I always meant to give you diamonds
(though Penny would not have wanted diamonds).
But you still wear a plain gold band
That old river keeps on rolling
We don't know just what's in store
But in spite of all of this
I don't love you like I did
I love you so much more.

OLD LOVE[1]
Neal & Leandra

It was the beginning of another phase of our lives. Pen overcame the death of her mother in 1991, and went on to abate her uncertainty in starting a private home practice of therapy clients. Our home was situated in an area of stillness and beauty, a little more than a mile from our church and from an outstanding food co-op. Three miles to the north was the upscale town of Wayzata and three miles to the southeast was the down-to-earth, but quaint town of Excelsior—both on Lake Minnetonka. It took only a few minutes to arrive at The Marsh, a state-of-the-art fitness center, a phoenix rising from the natural grasses around it. In this setting, we felt comfortable in being ourselves. Who we were shaped two unique views about the same topic, adding strength and zeal to our union.

The Marsh

David: We joined The Marsh, a center for balance and fitness, and enjoyed yoga, Pilates, massage, lap swimming, and basic exercise equipment. Set in a wild wetland area, the center provided a pleasing environment for communing with nature. Even in the winter months, we remarked about its beauty. Most of the birds had migrated, yet Penny noticed a few hearty ones remained. To make sure these birds had enough food, she methodically brought birdfeed and left it on the deck in back of the

The Marsh: view from the deck; Minnetonka, Minnesota

dining room. Another Marsh regular, Steven Polansky, noticed Penny's unusual, but compassionate behavior. Steve and Penny became friends. Originally from New York, Steve was a retired professor of literature and creative writing at St. Olaf College in Northfield, Minnesota. He had a great sense of humor, occasionally using Yiddish words, and we became good friends.

On Saturdays and Sundays in good weather, Pen and I would sit on the back deck of the center, quietly drinking our coffee or tea. Barn swallows that returned year after year would swoop, and we would talk about how good life was.

Penny: The snow has fallen all night,
          light, sleepy stuff.
          Grey dawn settling now over
          the marsh. I stand at its
          edge, holding a bag of crumbs.

       In front of me, the marsh looks
          mostly like so many white
          quilts, though tall stalks stand
          up to the snow, leaning every
          which way. The wild crabapple
          bushes look like rosy-cheeked
          children stooping close
          to the lace and white of the snow.

       This is a garden, of course, but
          this is a garden with a purpose.
          It must watch the rising of
          the sun and the moon, listen for
          the deep movement of roots and
          the call of even a single bird.
          And, it must ripen with the silence.

       "The Marsh—A Winter Morning"
       January, 1998

The North Shore

David: In the summer, we also loved to vacation at the North Shore of Lake Superior, staying near the picturesque town of Grand Marais. We hiked in the morning. Then, leisurely strolling the town, we'd stop at The Trading Post, Sivertson's Gallery, and the World's Best Donuts for coffee and a pastry. In the afternoon, Pen napped while I went for a run. Paradise Beach was our favorite spot because it was so secluded— tranquility at its best—just the two of us, absorbing the majesty and wisdom of this ancient lake.

Penny: Stillness—
and dull chant of waves,
light on everything,
squeezes between rocks
which are hot from the sun.

I pick one up
to warm my hands.
Sky, a blue dome.

No one but us
on the beach which is not sand
but small rocks
hard to walk on.

Oh, the stillness
which is not like emptiness,
more like our quiet
bodies as we walk,
more like the single
white gull who follows
us down the beach
on foot.

"August—Walking the Shore of Lake Superior"
August, 1997

Our Cats

David: Lamb Chop accompanied us on some of our North Shore vacations. Penny was often concerned that she would get overheated in the car while we had breakfast at one of our favorite restaurants, Cassidy's. During one such visit, I was enjoying my usual breakfast of eggs and oatmeal with fruit when Penny disappeared. She returned minutes later, carrying Lamb Chop. I was a little shocked, knowing that the restaurant did not allow animals on premise. Almost immediately, a very burly young man approached us, flashed his badge and said firmly, "You can't do that, ma'am." Penny passionately explained the dangers of high temperatures for pets whose owners had to leave them in cars. Naturally, this was not sufficient justification for violating restaurant policy or health department rules. The three of us made a hasty, yet respectful departure. Cassidy's has always been a favorite junction for Minnesota State Police officers.

Penny: I put my book on the table,
           turn out the light.
     Sam the cat
           jumps on to the bed.

     By moonlight,
           I see him turning from whisker
           to tail.
     He is making a perfect circle with his body,
           Turning once,
               twice,
           three times.
     He is making a place for himself
           in the tall grasses of my quilt.
     He is making a place for himself in the countless
           numbers of things on this earth.
     Now he circles down into a yellow and white
           ball, leaning heavily against the side of my body.
     He purrs.
     He sleeps.

     I make a place for myself in the mysteries
           of sleep.

I purr.
I sleep.

"Sam the Cat"
February 6, 1996

Humor

David: We had precious routines, rituals, and silly, inside jokes. Friends said that we even had our own language. A line we both used many times originated from *Seinfeld*. It came from a TV segment where George Costanza was trying to promote a crazy scheme to a delegation of Japanese business people. Soon tiring of George's obvious exaggerations, the head of the delegation said simply, "You go now." Whenever I was having fun being annoying to Pen, she would say, "You go now, Bro." In other situations, we both pantomimed the "poor soul" routine,[2] based on the Jackie Gleason character who tried, but could never quite get a break.

Penny: I want to be boring today;
        Let my stomach hang out,
    Let my back curve into a "C,"
    Be an old woman carrying bundles
        of sticks or groceries, or
        live rabbits on my back.
    But now, I have defeated myself.
    There can be nothing boring
        about live rabbits.

Journal entry
October 31, 1995

The Homecoming

David: My arrival home from work was one of the highlights of Penny's day. I knew the minute I stepped in the door, Penny would yell from around the corner in our family room,[3] "Bro. Bro." And I would return her exuberance, "Penroe. Penroe." Next I dashed upstairs to shed my suit coat, tie, and briefcase and rushed back to join her in the family room.

"The first duty of love is to listen," a quote from Paul Tillich, best described what followed. "Tell, tell! What is the state of the Bro?" she asked, the precursor to my debriefing the day. Penny was a good listener even though much of my work day screamed of stress. After our chat, Penny would make dinner and leave me to further unwind by playing piano or watching TV. In later years, it became our habit to enjoy a weekly dinner out, almost always at The Good Earth restaurant in The Galleria, Edina.

Friday evening's entertainment was listening to *Wall Street Week with Louis Rukeyser*. Finances came alive under his showmanship. Interested in being knowledgeable about the complexities of our investments, Penny sometimes pleasantly surprised me with her grasp of investment jargon. For example, she understood price-earning ratio (P/E), a formula that measured an investment's earnings against its share price.[4]

Penny: You have been listening
                  all your life —
                  to summer, when the sun
                  beats down on your back
                  like a drum
              to cold,
              creeping under your door
              with a sigh,

              to animals
              come back to
              happy fields again in March.

              For listening
                  is a sacred art,
                  like music.

              It is a sacred art,
                  this listening,
                  like music.

              "Bird's Birthday"
              2004

Rituals

David: Every evening by 9 P.M., Pen had a standing date in bed with The *New Yorker*, a publication she subscribed to for as long as I knew her. She enjoyed this quiet time by reading articles of interest, usually related to current events; cartoons; and *all* of the poetry.

Ideally, she didn't want to be disturbed while reading. However, not one to let a challenge go by, I sometimes would sneak into the bedroom on my belly and then pop my head up for a second or two. Penny would pretend I wasn't there for as long as she could, but then I would see a little smile cross her face. She knew I was being playful…and annoying. With a bit of importance in her voice, she would say, "Bro, you go now."

Penny: I have just finished reclaiming my house after a relative's visit. It feels W O ND E R FU L! How I love the solitude of woods and cat company. I am beginning to hear my own thoughts and feelings again.

Journal entry, excerpt
September 24, 1996

Weekends

David: We looked forward to our weekends when we would have more time to spend together. We usually went to Wayzata on Saturday mornings where Pen would look in the shops, and I visited the hardware store or library. Then we'd meet for coffee and a pastry. Occasionally, we were more adventurous and visited the International Design Center in downtown Minneapolis. It was a store that sold Scandinavian furniture and art, located in an old warehouse building that had a lot of character.

While Penny took a nap after lunch, I had time to complete odd jobs around the house and go for a run. Sometimes we went to movies, being especially fond of the $2 tickets at the Dock Theater in Excelsior. Penny also liked the "feel good" detective programs that had positive resolutions like *Perry Mason* and *Murder She Wrote* with Angela Landsbury.

Once in awhile we attended a concert that featured Bill Staines, Arlo Guthrie, or Pete Seeger. Penny loved dance performances, especially those of Bill T. Jones, during which I learned to appreciate an expressive art form combined with athleticism. On the weekends, we enjoyed the long winters by running outside, regardless of the conditions. We welcomed the changing of seasons with their attendant rituals—cleaning windows and opening up the house in the spring and gardening in the summer. Fall brought cleaning out gutters and putting up storm windows.

Penny: I could stay all day
        watching the wind move
        the leaves.
        It's like Sam, our cat,
        when he sits in quiet,
        then leaps and turns
        in the air.

    The garden waits
        for a human hand,
        ragged but still full
        of the sparks of life.

    In a month, I will
        cut and cover the flowers
        with dried leaves.
    This is for protection
        and a kind of blessing.

    Since we came together
        in this house, the house
        has grown. Children have
        pushed out the walls
        and windows, have finally
        flown to places within
        their own mind's eye.

    The walls, by now,
        are almost gone.
    We have finally moved
        to the woods where
        we began, knowing now

enough of love to
hold its true nature.

"14th Anniversary in a Second Marriage"
October 12, 1999

The sun.
    I am sitting on a deck chair
        in back of our house—
    The sun streams into my
        face, my arms and legs,
           my torso, my fingers and toes.
    It fits me like a glove.

    It takes away all thoughts,
    insists on total surrender.
    My concerns,
        like so much junk in a
        wheelbarrow, are carted away.

It leaves my breathing softly
    and totally in love with
    the sun.

"Things that are Close"
July 31, 1995

Who can know where the wind goes
    or the sweet air of Autumn?
Who can see the light left behind
    young foxes running silently
    through the pines?
Can you hear your heart speak?
Nothing is ever lost.
Listen.

Christmas Collection
1987

Chapter 10
The Rare Gift

Penny's observations about dying and death teach readers how to live. Much information is available about this physical process, yet the topic still mystifies most and makes them uncomfortable. Penny's words invite readers to reconsider dying and death as a natural part of the life cycle. This way of thinking promotes acceptance, rather than fear, and encourages honest conversations.

Penny's poems offer additional ways to understand death and dying that can serve as catalysts for people to live richer lives. Individuals become witnesses to others, offering them acceptance, mindful engagement, and peaceful temperaments. Witnesses who recall thoughtful conversations of life add tranquility and reassurance to the end-of-life experiences of loved ones.

For the most part, it is easy to connect with loved ones when things are going well. Even so, most people have difficulty sharing their deepest feelings about life. As compromising situations broadside lives, conversations become increasingly more difficult. Suffering loved ones may feel scared or confused, rise to "performance," or refuse to connect altogether.

Family members, caregivers or friends may react by suddenly becoming frustrated with or demanding of loved ones, only later to feel guilt or anger. Sometimes they regard loved ones as young children, telling them what to do. These same may rush in, judge what is happening, and try to fix the circumstances, not actions that demonstrate mindful support. Ironically, most important and helpful at this time is a quiet physical presence and the desire to listen, paying attention to expressed needs. This is the rare gift.

Individuals may prepare for end-of-life times or other challenging circumstances by becoming more present with their loved ones right now, day-to-day. Genuine inquiries about life stories, pictures, humor, and dreams will result in shared trust and wisdom. Then, when difficult times arise, people will better understand their loved ones, and loved ones will experience peace.

The time surrounding dying and death is not about mourners — as difficult as it is to hear and accept — it is about the loved ones who are making their transitions. It is easy for family members or friends to judge circumstances as good or bad, right or wrong. However, it isn't until people decide to focus on their loved ones that the loved ones actually feel safe in sharing their personal views. By focusing on conversations that engage loved ones' innermost thoughts, individuals can accurately determine the real feelings of loved ones. This is the first step toward being mindful.

When visiting with loved ones, it is essential to look really deeply into them--their eyes, bodies, and hearts. Regardless of the appearance of the physical body, souls of the loved ones remain healthy and intact. The energy of the soul is constant throughout time and space and, although physically unrecognizable, hears and understands all. Quietly being with each other in silence and feeling the connection of love maximizes the overall experience. Verbalizing feelings, if desired, increases impact. Nothing is ever lost.

Eddie, Penny's step-brother, thought highly of Penny. She and David were fond of him and his wife, Fran. Since both couples had second homes on Siesta Key, all of them connected during vacations. A highly successful stockbroker, Eddie passed away in September 2005 of post-operative complications following cardiac arrest.

A turning point, death brings family and friends together. Without negotiation, it provides an appointed moment in which survivors can step out of their usual responsibilities, honor loved ones, and reflect on the meaning of life and relationships. Hidden feelings often come forward, triggering deeply-concealed grief.

Some of Penny's most personal grief is symbolized by the biblical Rachel in the next poem. Like Rachel, Penny wanted children. Ironically, both women had a deep inner knowing that they would not live to see their children grow old or to support them throughout the trials of life.[1]

Sharing feelings and spending time with loved ones throughout a lifetime have the potential to enrich the time surrounding dying and death. How might meaningful conversations to discover the true feelings of loved ones during the living years lead to fewer guilty moments at the end of physical life?

> The phone rings.
> We drive from Minneapolis
> to Chicago,
> find the room
> where Rachel weeps
> and sit down.
> One death conjures up others
> like a magician drawing forth
> Birds and countless flowers
> from his sleeves
>
> and these others
> sit in a circle around us
> in hospital gowns or street clothes
> or proper black funeral suits
> in their stillness
> and we wonder
> if even the long silences
> must be loved.
>
> "Eddie"
> June 6, 2006

Often two people connect without words. They have grown to recognize each other's singularities: a listless sigh, a knowing glance or a light touch.

Nature mirrors their understanding. To those unfamiliar with the ways of the heart, subtleties go unnoticed. However, those who regard the moment and receive its gifts know gratitude. Connection deepens. Right now, what actions might demonstrate a heartfelt viewpoint or increased commitment to a relationship?

> A man and a woman walk
>   in the wide and high fields,
>   familiar to them
>   with the small, yellow
>   buttercups on the edges, and
>   covered by the endless sky.
>
> Now, in early September,
>   hundreds of Monarch butterflies
>   have come to the fields
>   of goldenrod. The butterflies
>   are temporary residents,
>   as are the man and the
>   woman, on this earth.
>
> Nothing in the fields has
>   changed, but the distant trees
>   have a knowingness
>   about them, the songs of
>   birds have softened.
>
> The man and the woman
>   talk and do not talk. They
>   are not old, but old enough
>   to know they will not always
>   be together, to know also
>   that the Monarchs, orange
>   as the lavish pumpkins — soon
>   to be cut open by children — will
>   also vanish.
>
> But now the herds of
>   Monarchs light on the

fields of goldenrod.
The ocean of them is as
wide as the man and
woman can see.

"September and the Monarchs"
September 2, 1997

Penny chose to see beauty in everything. Far more often than anyone knew, she imagined what death might be like. A blessing, her writing shared the cycles of the natural world, and through those observations, she developed a greater degree of trust. Her words speak of the unknown. Readers' hearts are light, rather than intimidated. Her creative mind painted nature scenes of the most pleasing surroundings for her loved ones who had made their transitions. At some profound level, she knew that everything in the universe was connected. How might this realization change human behavior?

I'm sure death is a rhythm, a
melody, like the cadence of the
deer running through the fields,
through the plain land of grasses.
They run before dawn, before the
cars and semis travel close to these
same grasses.
It is possible to hear death's song
in the sound of stars, which are,
after all, dying and being born all
the time?
But I want a place for my father
somewhere around me.
Though it would be like him to want
to drive truck all day and all night
and it would be like him to want to
be near water, to watch the silver
bodies of fish or just sit.
Maybe death is like the water but you
breathe with your spine or your spleen.
My father would like that.

And my father would sing, sing with
      gusto and not much song. He would
      sing in the woods and by the water.
And when the stars come out,
      I will come, as a human child,
and we will sing.

"Singing Now — Father"
May 12, 1998

Weaving factual observations with magical creativity, Penny's writing demonstrated many similarities between humans and animals. Not only did words still her mind, opening it to greater creativity, but also her perspective presented a fresh world to others. Her writing, like her personality, offered substance and depth. Readers who take her work to heart also may find calm when faced with adversity, perhaps even discovering a trace of lightness or humor. What will it take, today, to let go of propriety and fear? What could fill that space?

... A warm October Saturday, the three of us sit around the kitchen table with Cokes. My grandmother [maternal] is short and stout, wears long, drapey [sic] clothes, and a small hat with a single, very long feather. I watch her small features almost hidden beneath jowls: the skin on her face and hands is the yellow of the fall leaves. Her eyes are blue which I love, as they are the exact color of my favorite aunt's. My mother's eyes and mine are brown.

... The Chicago police called my mother when my grandmother died. I was away at college. The police found a lot of money hidden in grandmother's room, $1000 under the mattress.

This morning I watch a portly and plumed pheasant strut in the snow. He walks back and forth, waiting for the rascally squirrels to leave the feeder. How beautiful he is with his fat, brown chest and long, colored tail feathers. For a moment I am sure what has become of my grandmother.

"Grandmother," excerpts
January 14, 1997

Many of our fondest memories surround four-legged loved ones; absence recalls their most endearing qualities. Penny's long-time veterinarian, John Hotvet DVM, commented that Penny was "a person who helped to teach me to share my innermost feelings on every level, so essential to all of us when dealing with life and death issues, even with our pets who never seem to live quite long enough."

Saying good-bye to a loved one or friend, although important, is not necessarily what people remember most. For Penny, what lingered was what she learned about love: Humility. Complete and unconditional affection and commitment. Forgiveness. Gentleness. Compassion. During the quiet moments, what memories keep us close?

It's October 21st.
Lamb Chop died at 10:05 yesterday morning.
By the end, there was no choice —
     Not for her
     Not for David and me
     Not for Sammy, her brother.

I want to write down what made her
unique as a way of keeping her
still with me.
     She had soft and long gray fur and
     when I gently rubbed her ears,
     they felt like velvet.
     She had the poise of a sphinx.
     When she looked at me with her
     green eyes, she spoke so clearly:
          -Tme to eat.
          -Open the door to the deck, please.

-This food is not to my liking.
-I'm tired.
-I love you and you are mine forever.

She loved boxes, to sit on or
curl up in, and tissue paper
and magazines. Actually, she had
an interesting relationship
with paper. Two years ago, she
completely chewed up the cover
of a book of John Updike's poetry.

She also liked to eat flowers.
When I napped or was sick, she'd
jump up on the bed, lay down
on my chest, nose an inch
from mine.

Lamb Chop was a beautiful and authentic
presence in our lives for twelve
years, deeply respected, appreciated,
and loved. I have a Lamb Chop-
sized hole in my heart.

Nothing is permanent.
Saying good-bye is not the most
important thing.
The important thing is what she,
and everything we touch deeply,
teach us about love.

"Saying Good-bye to Lamb Chop"
October 23, 2003

No relationships are exempt from shadows. Experiencing these less-than-perfect moments also creates an opportunity to extend love. Once a common thread is found in contrite situations, both individuals will benefit from a heart that sees past ego. A broader view over a number of years shows that every personal interface has contributed something to the growth of an individual. Often this revelation takes time to recognize and accept. So it was for Penny. Every ounce of creativity and anti-materialistic fiber that she held dear was equally challenged by her mother's single-mindedness of decorum, power, and appearances.

Two sets of circumstances helped the women to better understand each other. Both shared compromised eyesight: Helen, from old-age glaucoma, and Penny, from an aneurysm. Secondly, both were hands-on healers. Penny offered grounding techniques during David's bouts with anxiety, and Helen eased ailments of Bay Village Nursing Home residents. Later, as her glaucoma worsened, Helen requested that Penny place her hands over Helen's eyes for healing. What seemingly negative circumstances, when revisited, might awaken gratitude today?

> When my mother lost her eyesight, everything changed. This was partly because reading had been her passion and partly because her whole body started giving out. She was tired all the time.

> She instructed my [step-] father to place her in a nursing facility so that he could continue weekly golf and not have to worry about her. My father visited her every evening and helped her eat her supper. Then they would chat.

> She lived for two more years in the nursing home. During that time, she told me that she cried almost every day, mainly about regrets. These were things she had done or things she had not been able to see and, therefore, do when her body was strong and eyes sightful. She said it was a good experience. My mother said she wondered if it had been necessary to lose her eyesight in order to see with her heart.

> She continued in the nursing home the practice of healing. The residents would come to her

room. She would sit on the edge of her bed [and] reach out her hands to them. Many people came. Apparently, seeing is not necessary to healing.

My mother said she was looking forward to "moving on and being done with this old body." She instructed me not to cry when she left, and I didn't at the cool Episcopalian memorial service.

I think about my mother and the mystery of a person's whole life. I wonder about how to prepare and finish this kind of work. I think my mother did a good job.

"My Mother"
November 2, 1996

Death brings roundness to the life cycle. It is inevitable and mysterious — a time of reflection and, often forgotten, a time of growth. Toward the end of life, loved ones often grow in courage, forgiveness, gratitude, and inner peace. Survivors receive the gift of time to process connections with loved ones, which may lead to the appreciation of unknown characteristics, talents, or dreams within a forgotten photo album. Greater understanding strengthens memories.

The little prince went away to look again at the roses.

"You are not at all like my rose," he said. "As yet you are nothing. No one has tamed you, and you have tamed no one. You are like my fox when I first knew him. He was only a fox like a hundred thousand other foxes. But I have made him my friend, and now he is unique in all the world."

And the roses were very much embarrassed.

You are beautiful, but you are empty, he went on. One could not die for you. To be sure, an ordinary passerby would think that my rose looked just like you — the rose that belongs to me. But in herself alone she is more important than all the hundreds of you other roses: because it is she that I have watered; because it is she that I have put under the glass globe; because it is she that I have sheltered behind the screen; … because it is she that I have listened to, when she grumbled, or boasted, or even sometimes when she said nothing. Because she is *my* rose.

"…It is the time you have wasted for your rose that makes your rose so important."

"…Men have forgotten this truth," said the fox. "But you must not forget it. You become responsible, forever, for what you have tamed. You are responsible for your rose…"

THE LITTLE PRINCE,[2] excerpts
Antoine De Saint-Exupéry

Those who continue in the life cycle might contemplate death as a continuation of energy in another, as of yet, unfamiliar time and space. As the end of the familiar physical body, death may also be viewed as the beginning of something new, a venture supported by perfect love.

As Penny viewed change through nature's eyes, transitions became possibilities: the courage of cilia peeking through the snow, tree blossoms becoming leaves or caterpillars emerging as striking butterflies. Amid endless time and changing forms, energy is constant. It is a powerful witness.

As we count time,
thunder is not even a step
behind the jagged line
of light in the night sky.
And as we count time,

I run from the woods
fast enough to leave
me standing here on the
front porch, cold, but dry,
watching the rain.
The garden will be washed clean.
Evergreens ready for sleep, though
they look the same as a month ago.
The pansies will die, of course,
and as we count time,
will be gone forever, unless
they bloom, purple and white
in another field without time.
What will you and I be when the snow
comes?
You, a bear, asleep by your desk?
Whatever animal I become
will take up its sadness
and whatever joy, and
come to the river, wait
there until snow fall, white
pansies that vanish on
the water.
If the animal of myself
makes a sound, it
will be a lot like singing.

"Cold Rain"
September 15, 1996

...in another field without time

Small, winged creature,
        I balance you on the smallest
        finger of my hand.
        Your wings are sheerer
        than the gauze that wraps
        your wound.
    There is goodness in this world
        as well as dark. Darkness
        holds the silent stars
        but goodness can't be held.
    Standing in this field
        with snow and open hands,
        I sing.

Christmas Collection[1]
1999

Chapter 11
Deep Knowing: A Monologue

Change crept surreptitiously into uncharted territory, determined to have its way. Penny's inner knowing, fully three years before an actual medical diagnosis, met with greater acuity on all levels: physical, mental, and spiritual. Without drawing undue attention, Penny instinctively knew that her heart's song and her body were at odds. She moved through this heightened awareness, sharing details only with her notebooks.

As a therapist, Penny was familiar with The Five Stages of Grief[2] as described by Elisabeth Kübler-Ross in her 1969 book, ON DEATH AND DYING. Penny most likely addressed similar phases of change with her clients. Yet suddenly, the question became personal: How to extract every ounce of life and its meaning out of time?

Denial

        I am up before 6.
        The sun already warm,
        marks its territory
        of lacy light
        on the grass.

The birds are quiet.
It's so still.
My mind circles around this
stillness
and lands on
the great thinkers:

Hagel, *Stillness*
will become thunder
of avalanche,

Proust, from his airless room,
muses, *Stillness*
exists only in the mind.

But Einstein,
old man with drooping socks
and wild hair, white
as the stars;
Stillness is the light itself.

"Einstein"
        June 29, 2001

Considerable angst over losing my billfold this morning (it had fallen between the front seat and the brake handle in my car). The loss threw me off center like a wild pitch. Actually, I wasn't even in the ball park. The closest thing to me would have to have been the ball—wound up tight, flying in some undetermined section of sky.

This is not a new sensation. Does everyone have this same malady? Loss of an important object spins us out away from our familiar self, bringing fear and disorientation. [It's] so hard for me to accept loss graciously.

Karen's birthday was warm and even jolly. I am surprised at my joy at being alone with my children. There were rough spots in my parenting, and I am sad when I remember things undone with and for my children.

But I also remember happiness and solidarity. I am impressed with each of them. They are each doing a good job of being themselves.

Journal entry
April 9, 1996

I am trying to learn to love people.
This work is like wedging myself
through the eye of a needle.

There are excuses of course,
being first raised as a daisy
and then as a rose and I have learned
how to love both daisies and roses.

David has been my primary teacher —
over many years by his loving me.
It is as clear as the smallest church bell
or the ring of a piccolo.

I do love the snow coming down today and the trees,
the grey and orange squirrels now running
in the snow, back and forth, by the woodpile.
And the night coons with their bandit eyes and
the deer who are so beautiful, standing in the
twilight by the feeder, all birds,
yellow Sam, our cat.

These I can see.
I am not able to love what I cannot
see.

I think there will be a time when
loving has nothing to do with
seeing —
Then I feel sure that the music of a
bell and
the sweetness of a piccolo, though
not seen,
I will love.

"The Piccolo"
January 25, 2007

All week I have missed
appointments, four so far
and it's only Wednesday,
none by my choice.
I have found myself
keeping appointments with
silence which has turned out
to be a good companion.
You might think it boring,
    but in the kindest of ways.
    I have been brought to
    the windows that lean out
    into the green woods.
    I have seen the birds filling the
blue sky
    with themselves,
    doing the most winsome
    of dances.

"Appointments Missed"
October, 1997

Anger

I am not myself today.
Another person has slid
into my body, silently,
while rain falls on
  the high house, its
  roof touching trees.
  We've lived here for years
  in good times and bad,
  where wind crouches
  down, blows big into
  corners of this house.

When you leave, or what
  passes for leaving, I
  will look for you,
  around the house,
  by the woodpile, in
  our stalky garden
  while rain washes the
  branches of naked trees
    'til they
gleam white as bones,
'til their roots deepen
and tangle.

"Rain in February"
September, 1998

It is still cold and cloudy.
I notice sadly how few song birds
  have come back; our three new
  bird houses are empty.
I feel empty, too.
I think I want a perfect world.
It is so hard to trust that there is
  something unique inside me,
  so hard to risk that it's there
  by exploring it.

This conversation with myself reminds
me of the workshops I did with Kirsten—
How "sure" I was of that kernel of
uniqueness each person has. How ephemeral
it seems now.
I want someone to take the sick feeling in my
belly away—to make my breathing full,
robust—to take away the fear.
But no diversions this morning.
Sweet Jesus, grant me courage.

Journal entry
May 7, 1996

...I am sitting in my warm room writing this,
feeling detached, resistant, even angry that I
trust so little what's inside me and my ability
to urge it out. I trust so little that anyone cares.

I look into the woods. There is a very tall and
old tree, taller than any of the others, casting
its slim and elegant shadow on to the snow. It
does not complain about feeling unappreciated.
It simply lays down its long, graceful shadow
in the frigid sunny morning, gently lays its
shadow down in the snow.

Journal entry, excerpt
March 26, 1996

Bargaining

It is clear fall is coming. At night we pull up
the quilt, but we still open windows and the
sliding screen door to the upper porch.

...I noticed two days ago that the barn swallows
have all left the marsh—not exactly without
a trace as their bestickled, circular homes are

still stuck to the corners of buildings. I miss the barn swallows very much and miss especially watching them swoop and glide in the sky above the wide, sunlit fields of The Marsh.

It is amazing to me that there is so little interest on the part of people in the comings and goings of barn swallows at The Marsh. Each person to whom I lamented their loss first looked surprised, then bored, then shifted weight from leg to leg in silence. What is it with people?

So this morning I am preparing my inner space for a change—I am looking for ways to move in cadence with the natural world around me. Right now, my only tools facilitating this movement are observation, mourning and blessing each loss as it comes, and letting go.

Journal entry, excerpts
August 29, 1996

I am beginning refocusing my energy and time. This is in response to an internal shift. I cannot at this time describe the shift or predict what will come through it. I know that the first thing I must do is take myself out of a variety of activities and involvements.

What I will keep is singing in the "regular" choir. That stays because it moves and nourishes my spirit. Nature also does this and being alone with the cats and writing. So, I will call Libby today and state my need. I also want time with David and my grown children.

Journal entry
November 20, 1996

I'm tense and spinning today—I want to take off the pressure I feel by doing, the way I medicate pain.

...I love what someone said about the Buddhists welcoming adversity. So, I am trying to be a Buddhist.

...My task is to accept the joy and the darkness. They clearly are two sides of the same coin. I will welcome them as graciously as I can.

Journal entry, excerpts
May 6, 1997

It's late.
The house is still.
The summer birds,
warblers & swallows
have gone to sleep,
each under a wing
or a leaf. I hear
their silence
through the open
windows & doors.
I look over at you,
silent as a Pope, reading.

Come lie down with me.
        Sing to me.
        Sing "Sweet Low."
        Sing "Sweet Adeline."
        Sing in your long, low voice.
        Sing as though nothing
        could ever harm us,
        not inside or out—
Sing the sound of wind
through these cedars
who stand also long
& silent in the dark—
rooted & full of life.

"I Asked My Husband to Sing to Me"
July 10, 2002

Depression

My house is full of light.
The early sun makes the trees throw long
    shadows into the snow.
...Even though the sky is blue as a robin's egg
    and trees in the woods grow
    out of the snow like slender women,
Even though I love my chair
    in this silent, sunny house,
    I ask for mercy.
Hold me no longer in your frozen arms.

"I Don't Appreciate This," excerpts
March 26, 1996

The air is heavy and the sky is full of dark clouds.
It's cold and I feel rain coming.
I have some apprehension about meeting my new
client, Mary Smith,[3] at four o'clock today.
She is bringing her father.
I am also apprehensive about leaving home
Thursday morning for Phoenix.
It's hard to put that aside.

It's hard to bring fear in close to me so that it can be
tended to and spread out into the whole me.
It's hard to take something small, pointed, and
sharp and spread it out soft like the heavy, grey
sky.

I think this is about letting go and trusting.
It helps when I breathe deeply and picture in my
mind those who love me.

Journal entry
April 22, 1996

David and I walked to the beach yesterday, Labor Day, to say good-bye to the beach and to the semi-lazy days of August. August has been wonderful, felt like a gift of time and space. The difference in August was a lack of the pressure of "oughts" — ought to call friends to get together, ought to go to church, ought to work on cleaning up the house, ought to fertilize the garden.

August helped me realize how "oughted" I am — and how that negates really choosing. This is a problem because I also genuinely enjoy all the activities on my above "ought" list. The key may be to notice when I am no longer honoring something I am doing. How I long to be in the present. From the state of being present, comes awareness and aliveness to the world around and within me.

Journal entry
September 3, 1996

Acceptance

It's the Tuesday after the wedding — Tom and Kerri's — and it's a badly needed rainy day. It's a day alone which I haven't had for several days. Carl Jung says that all things are connected if you stand back far enough. I take some steps backward to see if I can find some connections. I come up with two long strands — the strand of love and the strand of mortality.

How strong was the strand of love as Tom and Kerri, sometimes through tears, promised to love each other "'til death do us part"? And, in the joy of the mystical union, how will their marriage survive the inevitable shadow of their deaths and what feels like everlasting separation?

How proud I was and am of my son—his struggles over the past several years and his clear triumphs in the present moment. How very dear he is to me and how our love for each other has grown and won out over separation, anger, mistrust, and loss. How precious is the time we have together?

And the cool rain that is freely given to plants and people and trees and the dry earth—is given freely and unmeasured in the moment, with no promises or regrets. The rain's way of giving is also part of this light and shadow…

Journal entry, excerpt
June 24, 1997

…I am not very old, but
I think about this.
A silly thing.
    I will miss my cats—unless,
    of course, the spirit form
    is able to lie between their
    two soft bodies in the cold
    winter nights.

And the trees
    of our woods—will my
    spirit be able to watch
day by day, the luscious green
leaves turn gold and fall down,
    leaving dark bodies of trunks
    as the wood's sentinels?

And David,
    will you be able to feel
    my breath when you walk in the

woods?

"A Love Poem"
October 23, 1997

Clear and rich
with stars.
A red fox frequents
　　　the feeder each night.
　　　I'll keep the feeder
　　　full.

I go out into the cold
　　　and the dark,
　　　lanterns in the sky,
　　　everywhere. Tonight
　　　I am afraid of nothing,
　　　not poor health,
　　　not loneliness,
　　　not poverty.
I have company of stars
　　　and in a near
　　　thicket rests a red fox.

"Winter Night"
December 18, 1998

December,
　　　time of waiting
　　　and they are back,
　　　the owls,
　　　in the woods behind
　　　the house,
　　　a flock of them.
I go
　　　outside into the woods,
　　　light snow
　　　beginning and twilight.
　　　They call and call,

then silence.
I wait.
　　Looking up,
　　I see the outlines
　　of their fierce
　　and beautiful bodies,
　　clawed feet.
And I
　　know owl spirit,
　　yours and mine,
　　owl hunger,
　　owl soundings,
　　owl silence.
Night falls.
　　I watch through pine branches,
　　the holy stars come out.

Christmas Collection
1996

And I know owl spirit

Once upon a time there was a woman who believed that everything had a spirit. When she worked in her garden, she conversed with the vines of green beans and the tomatoes whether green or ripe. She also spoke with all manner of flowers, paying special attention to the high hollyhocks as she had an especially warm place in her heart for them. She could remember making brightly-skirted dolls of the flowers when she was a girl, which she was decidedly not now.

She lived with her husband and cat along a creek. When she walked along the creek for exercise, she carried on conversations with the water, sometimes heated discussions. And when she went to town to buy supplies, she spoke pleasantly with the wheat flour as well as the bolt and a half of bright fabric she planned to purchase to replace the sun-faded curtains in the kitchen.

Journal entry
October, 2000

Chapter 12
Chrysalis

An owl, I was Penny's kindred spirit who instinctively sensed her innermost thoughts. Ours was the inner knowledge of understanding. Like her, I loved the constantly transforming woods behind the big, white house. In the evenings, I reached out to her with my distinctive eight-to-nine-note call, and she heard.

I startle from sleep.
A sound so close it could be in the room,
cat on the quilt at the foot of the bed,
stirs,

silence.
Again the sound:
an owl very close to the house,
on the roof or in the eves,
the sound again, unmistakable through the starry night.
I have no language to understand,
no language to answer,
to express my thanks.

Christmas Collection
1983

⌘⌘⌘

March, 1999

David and Penny return from their Santa Fe vacation. Three weeks later, Penny reports gastro intestinal issues.

Mid April, 1999

Internist appointment, diagnosis: Irritable Bowel Syndrome; recommends change of diet.

May 12, 1999

At annual Obstetrics and Gynecology (OB/GYN) appointment, physician discovers possible ovarian cancer; ultrasound takes place that same afternoon. Tests reveal a large, suspicious mass. Surgeon of gynecology recommended. David and Penny shift into crisis mode.

Even though our waking cycles were different, Penny's and my energies connected, and we were grateful. In contrast to others of my species, living in close proximity to humans was my nature. I waited in the denseness of surrounding trees for the couple to return from their New Mexico trip. Like a protected nest, their house was patient, breathing in the comfort of the woods. The travelers had visited college friends, and it was unlike

...the sound again, unmistakable through the starry night

them to be gone very long, especially when they eagerly anticipated the gifts of a new season.

The spring lamb declared the full cycle of life and welcomed these extensions of the southwestern sun. However, carefully concealed in the shadows of the woods lurked the March lion that, in six weeks' time, would snatch their hearts' desires.

> How to ever
>   heal this evil—
>   This great
>   Evil? Unanswerable
>   question—
>   question without
>   size, without
>   dimension like
>   birth and death,
>
>   question from a
>   strange hand,
>   near as the happy
>   birds, sounding and
>   singing in this early
>   light—question,
>   murky as the human
>   heart.
> But, I can tell you something:
>   This morning I am strangely happy.—
>   The marsh lies like a sleeping
>   woman before me—
>   cat-tailed and tattered—
>
>   sumacs, reeds, daisies,
>   wilting grasses,
>   all in their stubby beauty,
>   prepare for sleep,
>   have no questions.

"Untitled"
September 20, 1999

The woods are creaking with cold.
something ahead of me moves,
    is still,
    half hidden in twilight, but I
    feel the huge body, legs
    slender as willow branches,
    eyes sunken from scarcity.
    The only sound — a heart
    beating wildly.
I do not know the inner meaning
    of things.
    Does mystery have shape and
    size, scent and sound?
    What is invisible in
    what we see?
This curious world —
    its sweetness and dread —
    What holds us so gently
    in the dark?

Christmas Collection
2000

Instructions
are on the white wall,
small and black: *Place one card…*
I can do this
most days
be the gambler
with green shades and dark glasses.
Make something
of what's been dealt
or having the good sense
to turn everything in-
ask for 5 new cards.
But in the end,
play,
even with impossible odds.

Which,
after all, is a holy thing:
much more amazing
than being 5 places at once.

"Place One Card in Each of 5 Places"[1]
May, 2001

⌘⌘⌘

May 13, 1999

David contacts one of his clients, an urologist at Mayo Clinic in Rocherster, Minnesota. She recommends getting in touch with one of two highly-skilled gynecology surgeons on staff.

May 14, 1999

Penny and David meet with Karl Podratz, M.D. Ph.D. and a surgical resident, Dr. Catalin Jurnalov. The couple learns that the chance of the mass being something other than ovarian cancer is extremely remote. Penny's CA-125 (tumor marker) reading is 1891; normal range for this marker is 0-30. Dr. Podratz states that when he started his surgical residency, average survivorship for this type and likely stage of Penny's cancer was less than six months. "Now, it's over three years," he announces. Surgery is scheduled for 7:45 A.M. on May 19.

May 19, 1999

Penny and David report to the surgical waiting area at 6:00 A.M. A staff person warmly greets Penny and transfers her to a wheelchair. David shares that they have lumps in their throats, yet look into each other's eyes. He says, "You're gonna make it through this, Penroe." Pen answers, "OK, Bro." Penny is scared, yet also determined to survive.

Penny and I shared a common essence, and our communication was based on a similar gift—the ability to see deeply, beyond the masks of life, into the heart of the matter. It was time to draw on mutual strength and take action. Although David's voice had a definite urgency, Penny's voice echoed a deeper knowing and emotional detachment that this was the next step along her life's journey. Wisdom told me that David and Penny would manage any calamity; they focused on the positive side of circumstances.

We come in twos and threes and alone
Through the snow and twilight, silently,
To this place where things begin.
You call through the silence,
I answer—we all answer.
And a kind of music begins
    that reaches the swallows
    nesting in the eves,
That reaches even the ugly,
    the lonely place,
That reaches the watchers
    who cannot be seen but sing also.
Now the perfect circle
    of a yellow moon, rises.

Christmas Collection
1985

Night has released itself
into this field.

After various years,
so little I understand.
Not nearly as much as the old
moon that hangs like a question
mark

in the deep sky.
Not nearly as much as these high

pines
that stand between us.

"Untitled"
March 27, 2004

They watched the sky
    until they were part
    of the night,

these men of royal blood
and human hearts.

They walked in the starlight
farther than they
ever thought they could

listening to the sounds
of the sheep on the hillside,

listening to what could
never be spoken.

"Three Men-2"
2000

⌘⌘⌘

May 19, 1999

    Surgery commences. Penny's daughter, Karen, waits in a
designated room; David waits in the chapel, imaging Penny
in healing light. After three to four hours, a staff member
appears and reads a list of family names, followed by room
assignments. Penny's name is not on the list.

    An hour later, David and Karen are given a room number;
they learn that they will be able to see Penny soon. After a
forty-five minute food break, David returns to yet an empty

room. Alarmed, he wonders if something has gone wrong. A nurse informs David and Karen that they can see Penny in the Intensive Care Unit (ICU).

They find Pen in a futuristic setting, hardly recognizable — her face very puffy, her body attached to a multitude of tubes and sensors. They both break down. Penny survives over six hours of surgery. Dr. Podratz reports the surgery went well. "We had her upside down in there; her diaphragm had a sheen, indicating cancer cells. We scraped it." The name for this procedure is debulking, the removal of all physically-detected cancer cells. David and Karen both order Manhattans at dinner.

May 20-June 10, 1999

Penny's recovery begins. Dr. Podratz tells Pen, "We worked hard for you in surgery yesterday. Now we need you to work hard for us." Penny is relieved, but nauseous. The doctor refers to the condition as postoperative pancreatitis. Five – ten – fifteen days: the standard antiemetics don't work. Penny loses fifteen pounds, and David is concerned about the delay in chemotherapy treatment.

As a last resort to stop the nausea, Penny is given Thorazine, an anti-psychotic drug known to be especially effective against nausea. One day after returning from a break, David finds Penny delusional. She snaps her fingers saying, "Can't we get some room service around here?!" Nurses summon the physician on call, and she reduces the Thorazine dosage. Penny retains food and returns to her normal mental state. David and Penny press for hospital release.

June 12, 1999

As Penny and David contemplate leaving the hospital against medical advice, Dr Podratz reluctantly agrees, re-enforcing admonitions. One Computed Tomography (CT) scan, six prescriptions, a referral to a Minneapolis oncologist and eight hours later, Penny is released with the status of "partial disability" for six weeks.

My binocular vision settled on something rather charming...

Once home, Penny is so thin that her clothes no longer fit. David looks away as she dresses; it is too painful to see her this way. Yet, Penny *is* finally home in a peaceful setting.

June 19, 1999

David takes Penny to her first oncology appointment in a wheelchair; she is still too weak to walk very far. Chemotherapy is postponed until she gains more weight and strength.

After Penny's surgery, I intuited that her life in the hospital was anything but normal. As I peered into the glass-walled family room, Penny's usual chair was empty. Recalling her grace and magnetism, I sat in stillness with closed eyes as I waited for night to bring activity. Like Penny, I was influenced by the moon's energy except it manifested differently in her. Penny had a love of greenery, calming energy, and plans about how things should unfold.

Sharing her reverence for nature, I couldn't wait for her to return home. I recalled times that she would hum. Like me, she had a range of vocals that kept outsiders guessing. When Penny arrived home, I noticed that she smiled up at David, knowing that familiar surroundings awaited her. Under his care and supervision, it would take Penny another six weeks to stabilize to her normal weight.

One day, amid my usual naps, I noticed that Penny was sketching in her notebook. Curious, I spread my brown and white wings and flappred silently to a tree nearer the window of the family room for a closer look. My binocular vision settled on something rather charming.

There are dozens of birds on
the feeder this cold and cloudy day,
small winter birds in browns and greys.

They swoop around the feeder,
light on the ledge,

fly quickly up
beating the air with their wings.

Each a master of grace, sure of
its place in the universe.

Out of wanton desire to own
such a mystical creature,
I draw a bird-likeness on my pad.

I press my drawing against
the window so the birds
can see it.
Very little interest.

There are dozens of birds on
the feeder this cold and cloudy
day in December.
I sometimes see these birds
just before sleep, hear the
flutter of their angel wings.

"December Poem"
December 5, 1995

A kind of waiting
comes the way
pale moon waits

for its chance,
a candle for flame.
The deer

stands in leaf mottled,
snow speckled, shining
almost evening, only yards away.

She looks at me,

the season of killing
behind her,

a woman
in thick brown coat and cap,
she might wait

to catch a cab
after a concert.
In my own

brown eyes and coat,
I wait
with her.

"A Kind of Waiting"
December 6, 2004

Breathing is scarce.
I feel sick.
I am in this small, white room alone.
A young man in blue scrubs
comes in,
checks my vitals.

Then I see you and Karen.
You're floating around
in this small, white room.
Karen says something
reassuring.

I'm still sick when I get home.
I order a beautiful yellow and white
chiffon dress from a catalog.
I want to give a party.
I write a lot of letters.
I give money away.
I start singing in a choir.

I finish chemo.
I'm scared to death.
Master Gu, the acupuncturist,
says, "Your energy is wiry.
Be more happy."
The healer says, "Go into
the room you have seen.
Is it lighted?"

My hair grows back
And I fall more
in love with David and this
beautiful world.

The doctor tells me the blood
is bad.
More chemo.
I'm sick to my stomach
and my fingernails and
toenails turn yellow.

This illness is a house
I cannot leave.
My body smells peculiar,
makes strange sounds.

But I have made a home here,
Secured green plants and
two fine cats. At night, in the dark,
spirits come. Their breath
covers my cheeks like wind.
Good can come of this.

And now, in the morning as I wake,
I feel your long body —
sleepy, solemn, still, sweet
mending for me
what you can.

"This Illness"
June 2000

⌘⌘⌘

Summer, 1999

Penny undergoes chemotherapy with Taxol and Carboplatin. She accepts the medications well and steadily regains her weight. By December, her CA–125 reading returns to 12-13, well within the normal range. She is in remission. David does not ask about the statistical odds of Penny's long-term survival; instinctively, he knows they are not good. He is determined to find complementary therapies that could take her out of the statistical pool. By including alternative healing methods as a part of her healing regimen, he hopes to increase her odds of survival.

David seeks advice from a medical consultant, an impressively credentialed MD, PhD. The recommendation is that Penny take three supplements: Wobenzym N, a German anti-inflammatory; green tea; and maitake mushroom extract. Penny begins taking these and other supplements including colostrum, obtained from a Minnesota farmer.

Penny believes there may be benefit in receiving energy work. She continues acupuncture and later becomes a private client of Chunyi Lin,[2] a certified international Qigong master. She practices a healthy lifestyle of diet and exercise. David continues to search for additional therapies.

September, 1999

David interviews a number of cancer survivors and is encouraged. Some stories of healing seem like miracles. Most impressive is the story of Doris Schulte, diagnosed with aggressive Small Cell Lung Cancer and given six to twelve months to live. She begins getting her affairs in order, including making dresses for her grandchildren to wear to her funeral.

Doris learns about reports of apparitions of the Virgin Mary and of healings in a Catholic church in Medjugorje, Bosnia and Herzegovina. She joins a travel tour to that area and attends a healing service. A priest, with no knowledge of her health condition, places his hand over the exact location of her cancer. At the time of David's interview, Doris had been cancer free for over thirteen years.

I was heartened to see Penny thrive under David's care and humor. I knew that Penny felt most comfortable with the outdoors close at hand. Rejuvenated by familiar bird sounds, earth murmurs, and the majestic beauty of her favorite trees only a window pane away, she became one with the strength she needed. I watched as the natural world paid homage to one of its own. As two of similar energies, we both sensed encouragement.

...A week ago Thursday, a large and very beautiful owl perched on a branch of one of the large maples in the woods side of the house. He was no farther than 20 feet away, stayed there for a long time, facing me directly with his eyes closed. I have never seen an owl out of captivity at such close range. I was thrilled.

Journal entry, excerpt
February 2, 1996

Trees
now in full flesh
like buxom women.

September.
This pale morning sun,
lacy, licking, skinny, slant-eyed

sneaks,
curls, hick-ups
like a child dancing

around
these tall old men
of many lives, of many

suns
and rain and snow
lying heavy on their strong arms.

And
I have loved them
for all their years.

Is
there more
than beauty?

Is
there more
than pain?
The trees say there is
only presence.

"Outside the Window"
October 11, 2004

Creases in the earth sing,
these veins run from the center back
to my hand. So the
    earth has a voice and hums like
    a child might to herself, hum
    to sleep in a dark room.

On this clear morning,
the sky fills with blueness and birds.
Bare trees reach fiercely,
with their own sound.

And the sound rings and

tones through the dark:
> You are with us.
> With us.
> With us.

"Sing"
December 6, 1999

⌘⌘⌘

May 11, 2000

At an appointment with her oncologist, Penny learns that her CA-125 reading has increased significantly. At an earlier appointment, the same oncologist offers her unsolicited opinion in the form of what the couple believes is a medical hex: indication of a specific amount of time that a patient will live. The doctor's opinion is that available drugs will probably keep Penny alive for four years, a statement that has the potential to be counter productive.

Further responding to Penny's comment that she is seeing an acupuncturist, the oncologist remarks, "If you want to have someone stick a needle in your toe, it's all right with me." David and Penny respond to the arrogant comment with a decision to seek treatment elsewhere.

September 1, 2000

They travel to Cancer Treatment Centers of America (CTCA), in Zion, Illinois, for an exploratory meeting with an oncologist. The specialist tells them that Penny can beat her disease by combining high dose chemotherapy with a stem cell transplant. There is approximately 10 percent risk of death, plus the cost of the procedure—an estimated $250,000 to $500,000—is not covered by insurance. David requests CTCA data about the efficacy of the treatment. The couple continues to seek additional consultation, meeting with Dr. Leo Twiggs at the University of Miami. They conclude that neither CTCA data nor information from Dr. Twiggs supports the treatment. Penny and David decide not to pursue this alternative.

Compromised health slowed Penny's dance with life and gave her more time to contemplate. She continued to live her questions and write wisely about her feelings. Like me, she lived in the moment which kept reality in check.

> This field,
>   so full of sky
>   and endless stars.
> I have learned
>   through reading that all
>   space is round, as curved
>   as the back of a rabbit.
>   Such mysterious information.
> So will all things come again
>   to their beginning
>   like the white lilies
>   now sleeping under snow
>   in the front garden
>   and the long grasses
>   under my feet
>   that move and moan
>   like something being born?

Christmas Collection
2003

This small dog, the size of a cat, is standing on a table in a Caribbean coffee shop — an outdoor table. With her are a young woman and a boy. The dog is short-haired, black and white with huge ears for her size. She's got a cheery red color, black nose and eyes.

Well, she's beautiful.
I think to myself, if I had a dog like that, I'd take
her everywhere with me. I'd sew pockets in all my
clothes. I'd take her to the gas station and the
woods, to work and to church.

Then I stop and think, what kind of a life is that
    for a sweet, beautiful, small dog, living in
        someone's pocket? The boy is looking at me.
"Do you want to hold her?" he asks.
"I don't think so," I say.
I smile. The boy smiles.

The dog sits down on the table, then lies down on
    her belly, closes her eyes in the morning sun.

She has made me very happy.

I think it is better not to try to hold on to what
    makes one happy.

"What Makes Me Happy?"
June, 2000

I could
hardly hear.
The distance,

maybe a half mile,
so I walked toward.
Twilight rolling through

the wet field,
my shoes, wet
as two fish fresh from the sea.

I wanted
to find some

ingenious voice or rhythm
but when
I came to where
sound had been,

nothing but
silence,
silence as rich

and full as a Bach Fugue.
So I sang
while the night

enclosed me and
I wonder,
Will death

be like this —
Will it be
like coming

to a wet field
filled with
silence?

"Was it an Owl?"
August 25, 2003

⌘⌘⌘

December 6, 2000
> Penny and David meet with Patricia L. Judson, MD,
> Assistant Professor, Division of Gynecologic Oncology,
> University of Minnesota Hospital and Clinic (UM) on a
> referral from Penny's OB/GYN physician. Dr. Judson is
> bright, has excellent interpersonal skills and is well
> connected within the research community. Dr. Judson
> supports Penny's alternative and complementary therapy
> program, and they establish a good rapport.

February 14, 2001

> This date marks the first of many appointments with Dr.
> Judson over six years. As a practical matter, the level of care
> is excellent. The couple regards Dr. Judson; her assistant,
> Dona Maki; and the staff of residents as family. The
> treatment process becomes ritualistic. Penny has a monthly
> blood draw on a Thursday in preparation for the following
> Monday's appointment.

March-December, 2001

> Penny learns that her CA-125 reading is higher than
> the reading of the previous week. She calls David at his
> workplace. This elevated direction requires an adjustment
> in chemo protocol at the next visit. Dr. Judson seems to have
> another alternative whenever a change is required. Penny
> responds to nearly every chemotherapy drug (agent), even
> after the first round of drugs. Statistically, successive rounds
> of agents are effective for only 20 percent of cancer patients.
> She continues with Doxol longer than any other UM patient.
>
> Because University Hospital is a teaching facility, Penny and
> David often wait sixty to ninety minutes in the examination
> room before seeing Dr. Judson. That is a long time to be in a
> small room without windows. Always adaptive, David and
> Penny find things to laugh about.
>
> One time Dr. Judson appears in the room and smiles when
> she hears them singing. Another time, David asks the female
> resident who took Penny's initial information if she could do
> something about Penny's being so oversexed. A smile lights
> up the resident's face. Nothing could have been further from
> the truth.
>
> Penny continues her alternative therapy program. David
> and Penny attend a cancer survivor seminar led by Sid
> Levinsohn, who recommends using imagery for healing.
> Sid, himself diagnosed with cancer, interviewed many long-
> term cancer survivors over three years. He concluded that
> patients, even those whose cancer had metastasized, shared

a common thread: All had a deep CONVICTION that they would survive. The couple learns that having conviction goes beyond having a positive attitude.

I sensed Penny's continued valiant efforts to sustain her body, driven by her determination to find beauty in every situation. Her perspectives aligned with philosophies of other admired authors and poets. The mystical tone of her work added a soulful touch to her understanding of life.

As kindred spirits, Penny and I studied the details of our surroundings, assessed the situation, and moved into the unknown with confidence. Any other choice would not have been true to our hearts.

> Grey sky,
>> ground, bare, cold.
>> Birds shiver and flicker
>> near the feeder.
> What has come to me
>> has come,
>> leaving me to consider spirits;
>> around,
>> inside,
>> unknown and known.
> This is the gift
>> I have been given,
>> this crown of jewels,
>> blue, chartreuse, rose, yellow,
>> invisible to the
>> naked eye.
> Through this weakness,
>> I walk the grey ground,
>> the grey sky.
>> I wait quietly for
>> the snow.

"Untitled"
November 30, 1999

When I was 7, we lived in the
        house covered with vines
        and with a pointed roof.
        Sunday mornings my father
        whispered into my room,
        "We'll go to the woods."
Spring flowers were everywhere,
        purple, white, some shaped
        like tea cups.
        He walked ahead, fast.
        I could hardly keep up because
        I was watching the colonies
        of flowers coming into the light.

My father died when I was
        12, and I was one of the small
        animals that listened for the
        owl in the night.

Now I am old. I have
        this illness and go for treatments
        when my body is strong enough.

Sometimes, at night, there is the sound
        of an owl, sometimes the
        sound of my father's voice.

But this morning,
        the air is light on my cheek.
        I watch the marsh grasses
        beginning their journey
        into November.
        The barn swallows are
        sweeping the sky with their
        outstretched wings.

Journal entry
August 13, 1999

In the dark
>   my ears search for fox
>   who comes each night
>
>   padding between trees
>   spinning moon — light off his fur —
>   and where is coon?
>   But this poem is not
>   about absence,
>   but seeing
>
>   and what is closer
>   than the snow,
>   fuller than even
>
>   this shining field
>   with its stars?

Christmas Collection
2005

⌘⌘⌘

2002 to 2006

David continues to search for revolutionary cancer treatments that can help Penny. They schedule an appointment at Brock Medical Clinic, Evanston, Illinois. Dr. Brock believes that diet can make the body less hospitable to cancer. Penny begins following some of his recommendations.

David and Penny attend a Chicago seminar with Robert Jaffe, MD, who believes that there is a psycho-emotional source for all disease, the discovery of which is the first step to healing. Distance prohibits working with Dr. Jaffe.

David returns from work one day to find Penny doubled over in intense pain and notifies Dr. Judson. Penny is admitted to the University Emergency Room (ER) for tests.

She is jaundiced, indicating a possible liver issue. David is concerned about possible metastasis. Diagnosis: pancreatitis.

Penny complains of low back pain at a regular appointment with Dr. Judson. Tests reveal a blockage, due to swelling, and Penny is referred to Intervention Radiology. There, she receives a tube that drains fluid from her kidneys. David empties and sanitizes the apparatus twice a day. Later, periodic replacements of stents substitute for the tubes, making life much easier for both of them.

April 4, 2005

Penny has hip replacement surgery at Abbott Northwestern Hospital, a procedure unrelated to her ovarian cancer. She is released several days later.

November, 2006

Penny and David receive two urgent voicemail messages from University Hospital. The results of Penny's blood test reveals a serious fungus infection. She is admitted to the hospital and an infectious disease specialist is summoned immediately. Penny is treated and released within a week.

For several years, Penny's disease was under control. Like me, she craved more solitude and stillness. In between medical appointments, she observed and wrote. Trying to make sense of this time in her life, she recalled people, relationships and circumstances that evoked memories. Humorous perspective helped to distract reality just enough to get over the rough spots.

Penny rarely complained. Once in a while, though, David chuckled at her spunky and confrontational personality.

We met an oncologist who substituted once

for Dr. Judson. Penny called him by his first name, Uri.[3] She could tell he was very young and believed that he was not particularly knowledgeable about her medical history. Penny had first-hand experience with Taxotere at CTCA. In *her* case, it had little measurable effect on her cancer cells. As Uri touted the success of Taxotere, she completely rejected his advice. He said that it was too early to judge its effectiveness. Pen didn't believe him at all and said, "Yeah, but my CA-125 is up a f---ing 100 points!

After he left the room, I asked her if she shouldn't address him as Dr. Sokolov, given his credentials. Penny instantly quipped, "Well, he had his hand up my ass—I think I can call him anything I want!" That was my Pen.

"Fall"
2005

It's the end of August.
>   Every time I go to the store,
>   this fat, fledgling barn swallow
>   is sitting on the edge
>   of its twiggy nest—
>   too fat to fit inside.

>   Its parents swoop
>   around the parking lot,
>   looking, I think, for bugs.
>   He squawks and opens his
>   pink mouth every two seconds.

Why doesn't this big baby fly?
>   Give its parents a night out,
>   dinner and a movie?
The truth is:

163

leaving is hard on the spirit,
even little leavings—
throwing away your favorite, but
worn out jeans.

Bigger things—
slamming the car door as you
head for college
or leaving a friend
to take a new job in a new town.
You've walked together in the woods,
listened to the rush of waters,
to no sound at all.
Listened to its absence.

Maybe leaving for good
will be like that—
no sound at all

or maybe it will be like a
sunny morning,
like this one—

where one can stand on a
deck with one cat and
watch the birds
and the sun playing with the
high fields beyond the house

and nine crows on the grass
who are squawking and strutting
around.

"Cats and Birds"
September, 2001

I look down
at the blueberries
in the yellow colander
and see abundance.

I toss
them up
so each gleaming berry

comes under the stern stream
of the faucet's clear water.

I pick out
the green stems,
the mushy, collapsed ones.

they smell like hay.

July is their month —
time of
their fiercest offering —

not a sacrifice,
mind you,
but a gift.

Is this not true?

Ask your tongue
and the pink insides
of your mouth.

These fat, blue
mysteries,
are they not worthy

of eternal praise?

"In Praise of Blueberries"
July 21, 2004

January, 2007

While in Florida, Penny and David's beloved cat, Sam, is euthanized. They acquire another female orange tabby that was left among a litter on a vet's doorstep. David recalls the tears on Penny's cheeks as she held the kitten, Samantha. And he remembers thinking that he would probably live longer with Samantha than with Penny.

March, 2007

During a second trip to Florida, Penny has some difficulty with diarrhea, and David is concerned about metastasis. Dr. Judson prescribes Tincture of Opium.

August, 2007

David is diagnosed with low-grade prostate cancer. Concerned about staying healthy to support Penny, he schedules robotic surgery for October.

Early October, 2007

Penny is hospitalized for five days for intestinal issues and dehydration. After returning home, she asks David if he thinks she is going to die.[4] David answers gently, "Don't talk like that, Pen. Your tumor marker is not that high."

October 9, 2007

David undergoes successful surgery for prostate cancer with only an overnight hospital stay.

October 20, 2007

David and Penny decide to take a Saturday excursion to an Excelsior mall. Penny stumbles on an uneven brick surface and falls. "How much more, Lord? How much more?" David wonders and sees the same question reflected on Penny's face. It is the first time he sees her struggle with despondency. A clerk calls 911, and a team of emergency responders arrives. Penny resists going to the hospital, yet, when asked to stand, is unable to support her weight. Penny is transported to the hospital. Diagnosis: hip fracture, a devastating physical and psychological blow. Surgery follows that evening at Methodist Hospital.

November 6, 2007

David privately learns that Penny may not survive much longer, yet she might "surprise us," in the words of Dr. Judson. Only 50 percent of patients with hip fractures live for more than six months.

Mid November-Mid December, 2007

Penny is in and out of the hospital four times with treatments for dehydration and Clostridium Difficile (C Diff), a persistent bacterial condition. A home health care worker is assigned to manage Penny's dehydration.

As her dis-ease intensified, plucking both daisy and rose, Penny yearned for the energizing freedom that nature offered. Often she had felt it, had marveled at it, and had written about it. I, too, valued the liberty she longed for—the solitude of flight or a panoramic view. To compensate, she called upon her reverie: falling in love with the white mare; witnessing the rare gathering of Monarchs; walking with David in the moonlight as Lake Superior waves lapped endlessly over rocks; comforting a stranded, scared kitten while overcoming tumultuous conditions; and hearing my soothing call from the eaves in the middle of the night.

Owl has come
wide-eyed and wild,
conversing in the trees.

I know he is beautiful
but not subtle.
He did not bring this cold

but here it is.
Time is also here,
stern and getting sterner.

There were endless fields
in those days and from those fields,
a horse, old and sleek,
walked with me by the river,
ran to meet me,
put his old muzzle in my hand,
looking for a carrot.
That was a different person.

"In Those Days"
January 17, 2005

This is like wandering
in a strange land.
Walk slowly, though
my feet do not touch
the ground.

It's like those movies
of the 30s where the
hero, panicking because
his children are in their
beds asleep, sees fire fringing
slowly toward them.

If only my feet could
reach to solid earth
to be certain of
the dawn.

Illness
June 2003

The robins came on Valentine's Day —
30 or 40 of them
on the grass

in the front yard.
It hasn't rained here in weeks

so David went out with

a baking pan of water.
Some dipped their heads delicately
like kings or queens.

Others went whole hog in
with great splashing
and waving of wings.

By noon, the dry pan yawned
and smiled in the sun
as did we
sitting on the front porch as
the last of them headed North.

That afternoon,
I told my 102-year-old father
about the birds.

"They're passing through," he said
"as we all are."

"Robins"
March 25, 2004

⌘⌘⌘

December 22, 2007

David returns home to find Penny writhing in pain from
a colon spasm. The pain subsides, yet Penny is unable to
eat or drink, and David is concerned about dehydration and
kidney function. Penny resists going to the ER.

December 23, 2007

After a difficult night, Penny allows David to take her to the
ER. Diagnosis: bowel obstruction. Penny is hospitalized and
in the care of her oncologist. David worries about the latest
complication; believes the obstruction can be surgically

removed.

December 24, 2007

Penny is very alert and seems comfortable and at peace reading The *New Yorker*. By late afternoon, it is snowing heavily. Pen says, "Bro, you need to get going before this snow gets too deep." David replies, "OK, Penroe, I love you." "I love you, Bro." These are the last words David hears from Penny while she is fully conscious.

Death is not a topic that David and Penny openly discuss. Both prefer to keep a positive outlook, believing it will increase the likelihood of Penny's survival. David feels that Penny realizes her days are numbered. Uncharacteristically, Penny does not outwardly acknowledge this reality. David is not sure why, but he knows that for him, the situation is simply too painful to verbalize.

I associated nature's beauty and holiness with Penny. I felt her spirit incrementally release her body's physical trauma and its constraints. She had a new level of understanding where love and light began to replace suffering and uncertainty. An uncontainable knowing was born.

By the law of time,
　　we have been married
　　for 15 years.
　　By the law of the river,
　　we have become the water,
　　flowing and changing.

　　You have been kind to me,
　　have been the summer fields
　　for me to walk through,
　　for me to lie down and watch

clouds.
You have brought me in
when the snow came
and built a fire.

In this pocket of time, we
have been given, my soul
has rested and reached in
you and through you.
I am grateful and amazed.

If the spirit has a law, I think
it would be this shining thing,
this light covering everything,
everything.

"15th Anniversary"
October, 2000

Yesterday
I sat in stillness
by the woods and
one still spotted

and young deer
walked close
and closer, watching only
slender green shoots beneath her.

I did not
touch her, though
I could have,
nor reach out

a hand.
A kind of waiting
came over me —

the way

the silent moon
waits for darkness
and I understood

the holiness of waiting—

and time stopped
and two were
one.

"Deer"
September 21, 2004

Gather yourself like the damp quilt
    of the fog which works its
      way into the most intimate parts of you.
    Amen.
Dig deep roots and grow bark, brown as the
    earth where you will finally return.
    Amen.
In December, settle into the snow
    of you, lie on roof tops, lean
    against the sides of barns and
    houses. Walk the snow of you
    across the fields, through fences,
    all in silence.
    Amen.

Let the fox of you and the deer and
    the wolf come for warm winter
    coats. And in the spring, when foals are born,
    find the hidden places of you and rest.
    Amen.

When the dark comes, put on the
    heavy boots of you. Walk into

the clear night with its stars.
Walk on feet and paws, making the
sound that is your own,
that has no voice, but is heard everywhere.
Amen.

"Instructions on Prayer"
February 1998

⌘⌘⌘

Christmas Day, 2007

David returns to the hospital; Penny is undergoing a
procedure to change her stent. Nurses return her to her room
in a semi-conscious state. David inquires and is assured that
she has not been given too much anesthesia.

December 26, 2007

David is advised that all is being done to keep Penny as
comfortable as possible. He learns that Penny's bowel
obstruction cannot be surgically removed because her
colon, at this point, is most likely covered with cancer
cells and is no longer pliable. Dr. Judson returns David's
call from her home, expressing regret and confirming that
Penny can no longer be treated. David meets with a hospice
representative.

December 27, 2007

David makes arrangements for Penny's best friends to be
present when she arrives home by ambulance. Working
together, they move her to a hospital bed set up in her
beloved, glass-walled family room. Regaining consciousness
briefly, Penny exclaims, "Jay! What are you doing here?"
Friends Jo Bolte, Kirsten and Jay Johnson, Al Naylor and
Ann Woodbeck join David in celebrating Penny by singing.
And in her presence, love resounds.

December 29, 2007

     Jan Bach, Penny's good friend from Forrest, arrives to say good bye. Penny remains unconscious, although her soul registers his presence.

December 30, 2007

     Penny takes her last breath at 7:00 A.M. with David at her side.

Penny's writing offers wisdom, inspiration, beauty, and humor--a twist on the traditional. As kindred spirits, she and I may not have gained all of the insights hoped for (or had all of our questions answered!), yet living our mysteries was remarkable. We are grateful for the richness of exploration. Coming together, our spirits release all things worldly, and we become one with divine light. A single feather touches the earth.

> The soul is not blind
> like the lady meting out justice
> with her eyes covered with a cloth.
>
> But what does the soul see?
> Sunshine and rain?
> Flowers and trees?
>
> I am sure
> the soul sees light and dark and fog,
> feels wind and snow.
>
> The soul must hear silence,
> and the sound of animals,
> especially animals who are hurt.
>
> The soul sees most clearly,
> not exactly people
> but the results of people—

feels their breath
hears
their singing.

"What Does the Soul See?"
June 24, 2004

Spiney, prickly — belly
goes at the bottom
of blue and white Chinese bowl.

Then water.
I add each flower thoughtfully,
like sending children, one by one

into a garden
until the bowl is just filled
with daisies and spaces,

one necessary
for the other, like breathing
in and out.

Each flower,
different as snow flakes
while cold February sun

stretches and yawns
into the kitchen. I have
such excellent company.

"Arranging Daisies"
March 26, 2004

May I never not be frisky,
May I never not be risqué.

May my ashes, when you have them, friend,

and give them to the ocean,
leap in the froth of the waves,
still loving movement,

still ready, beyond all else,
to dance for the world.

"Prayer"[5]
Mary Oliver

The time will come
when, with elation,
you will greet yourself arriving
at your own door, in your own
mirror,
and each will smile at the other's
welcome,
and say, sit here. Eat.
You will love again the stranger who
was your self.
Give wine. Give bread. Give back
your heart
to itself, to the stranger who has
loved you

all your life, whom you ignored
for another, who knows you by
heart.
Take down the love letters from the
bookshelf,

the photographs, the desperate notes,
peel your own image from the

mirror.
Sit. Feast on your life.

"Love after Love"[6]
Derek Walcott[7]

Bitter cold January day
bright sunlight
blue sky,
this bird, large and dark,
comes to me from the woods.

Perches on a near branch,
opens eyes wide and beak,
says nothing,
watches,
waits.

I am motionless.
I stare at this fierce and beautiful
bird,
awed.

Resisting questions,
resisting desire,
I stay as simply as I can
with sun and sky,
with the mystery of this visitor.

"Owl"
February 2, 1996

After Penny died during the early morning hours of December 30, 2007, I left the house and headed to Carver Park to walk on a trail that we had walked on together many times. I was hoping for some kind of sign from Pen by way of the animal world—an owl landing on a nearby branch, a deer or fox coming close and stopping. Nothing remarkable happened that day. Yet the next day, a very large owl perched on a branch right outside the family room where Penny took her last breath. He seemed to be peering inside in broad daylight! I said to myself, I think that's my Pen. It would be the way she would choose to appear to give us a message that she is OK. Penny was known as a sage and had written poems about owls.

David
December, 2012

Epilogue
Part I
Honoring Penny

As I write these words, it is nearly seven years since the devastating loss to cancer of Penroe, my soul mate. I am learning to live with loss and to find inner healing. However, there will always be the emptiness, the hole in my heart that my Penroe will occupy in spirit. It is not a bad thing for it is the result of having a loving relationship of great depth.

I used to scoff at sympathy cards with messages about still having memories. *Yeah, great,* I thought, *all you've got left are the memories.* Yet, now I am flooded with them, and even though life can never be the same, they are precious. Although it is bittersweet to recall them, I remember them with a thankful heart.

A blur, the three-week period after Penny died and the day of her memorial service were exceedingly busy. I can't imagine planning a memorial service within a week of a loved one's death. A way to honor Penny and to say good-bye to her guided my planning. Setting up the service—held January 19, 2008, in Minnesota—proved to be a challenging time. Post-holidays, sub-zero temperatures, and navigation of ice challenged even the heartiest of souls.

Our four adult children helped in a variety of ways. Karen compiled, edited, and produced a chapbook of Penny's poetry with the assistance of our professional writer friend, Steven Polansky. Tom and Kerri assembled two pictorial displays of Penny's life. The presence and support of Meghan, Chris, and Steve was invaluable.

Working together with many talented friends uplifted me, and the day of the service became a moving tribute of loving words, music and gratitude—everything Penny represented. One of the highlights was a beautiful dance choreographed by Marylee Hardenbergh and performed by five of Penny's dance therapy friends. Randy Schumacher, our beloved long-time choir director, assisted with music selections and enlisted volunteers from the St. Luke Choir. They joined singers from the Wayzata Community Church (WCC); together they sang the touching old hymn, "Sweet, Sweet Spirit" and the contemporary piece, "You Are the New Day." Autumn Toussaint, a friend and an outstanding singer, performed "The Lord's Prayer."

I wondered how I would manage to bear my grief. The service was beautiful, yet I felt somehow that I was a distant observer. Pleased by the outpouring of admiration and respect, I felt, strangely enough, numb to deep emotion. Nothing had prepared me for this situation. I tried to be gracious and thank people for attending. Our friend, Reverend Sally Hill, commented that it was the most beautiful service she had ever attended.

Two more experiences would contribute to my getting closure. One was scheduling a meeting with Dr. Judson, Penny's oncologist. The other was scheduling Penny's Service of Interment for early spring in Sarasota, Florida, when Karen and Tom had planned to visit their dad on Sanibel Island.

Chris joined me for the debriefing with Dr. Judson at the University of Minnesota Medical Center. I had some lingering questions about Penny's medical situation. As soon as I started to speak about Penny, I was unexpectedly overcome with emotion. Dr. Judson said that my reaction was not uncommon. She clasped my hands as her eyes reddened. After regaining my composure, I asked about the blockage in Penny's kidney. Dr. Judson stated that it was likely a metastasis of the cancer athough she had not shared this with Penny or me at the time.

The Service of Interment was held in March of 2008, in the open columbarium chapel of Saint Boniface Church, only a mile from our home on Siesta Key. Reverend Wes Wasdyke officiated. Family members and nearly twenty of our Florida friends and neighbors attended. Together, we witnessed a simple, yet lovely service although the warm and sunny day seemed a little surreal as I sat there with Penny's burial urn. How had our wonderful life suddenly ended with such lightening speed?

Part II
Recalling bittersweet times

The support of family and friends fell away quickly as everyone returned to familiar life patterns. A week after Penny's memorial service, I drove to our place in Florida. The reality of losing Penny struck with ravaging force. In many ways Penny and I were one person, so it was literally like losing a part of me. I remember sobbing about every twenty minutes as I drove the familiar route past Madison, Rockford, and Bloomington to Paducah; through Nashville, Chattanooga, and Atlanta to Valdosta; and then past Gainesville, Ocala, and Tampa to Sarasota. I missed Pen singing the Illinois fight song when I crossed the border. I would challenge her, "Yeah, Penroe, I know how it goes," and she would persist singing even louder before we both started laughing.

I didn't want to change the Florida trip routine because it was so comfortable, yet it was difficult to stay in the places that Pen and I had frequented. It did not seem real to me to be there without her. I pictured her sitting across from me in restaurants, and that uplifted my spirits. I discreetly talked with her; however, if people thought I was schizophrenic, I really didn't care.

Feeling close to Penny comforted me. In the car, I draped one of her outfits over the front passenger's seat and placed a pair of her sneakers on the floor. Friends and family thought this practice was a little crazy, yet they respected my response to grief. This routine continued for over two years.

The beach on Siesta Key was the location of another one of our endearing times together. Except for Sundays, Penny enjoyed a daily walk on the beach at daybreak because her energy level was highest in the morning. I got up in time to drive her the half mile distance to the beach and drop her off at the public pavilion. We had a routine — some might think it silly — the memory of which still makes me smile. Pen acted hesitantly about getting out of the car. I think it all started on a day when it was windy, cold, and not very pleasant for a beach walk. She would say, "Bro, you mean I have to get out now?" I would say, "Yes, Penroe, it's time to get out now." She would continue to hesitate, and I would say in a firmer tone, imitating a line from a Seinfeld episode, "Penroe, you go now!" She hesitated even more, and I would finally say, "Penroe, get your butt out," all in fun, of course. With a face of amused defiance, she would get out of the car.

Meanwhile, I bought a newspaper, went home for a half hour to grab a cup of coffee, and returned to pick her up. I walked out on the beach to greet her, seeing her in the distance waving and yelling, "Bro, Bro!" For the first few weeks, I not only went through the motions of dropping her off, but also returned to pick her up. I stopped the return trips because I found them too painful, yet I continued the daily charade of our humorous drop-off routine for several years. Because I remembered our lines so well, the re-enactment consoled my heart.

The first six months after losing Penny were awful. I wondered to myself what I was doing, living on without her? It was a time of basic survival, hour by hour, day by day. I really didn't want to live. I compared life to running a race where I felt extreme pain as I tried to reach a non-existent finish line. I half-heartedly contemplated suicide; however, deep in my soul, I believed that life was a precious gift. I hoped that someday it would be worth living again.

I recalled the lyrics of the second verse to "Lonesome Valley."[1]

> We must walk this lonesome valley,
> We have to walk it by ourselves;
> O, nobody else can walk it for us,
> We have to walk it by ourselves.

I would not have wanted anyone else to walk my path. I needed and wanted to feel my pain. I had enjoyed a wonderful life and now I had to get through a rough patch, as Penny called it — a real rough patch. I needed patience, gratitude in all things, and grace. What doesn't break a person makes one stronger.

I handled this loss like I have dealt with other challenges in my life, methodically and compulsively. Embracing my pain, I intentionally returned to Fairview University Hospital on the second anniversary of Penny's death and walked past what had been her last room. I sobbed all the way home that day.

On one of my return trips to Minnesota, I stopped in Forrest, Illinois, to interview some people for Penny's biography. I met with Penny's friend and classmate, Kay Lindenbaum Crane, in her home. Kay was gracious and enthusiastically cooperative, as I had expected. I was feeling some sense of urgency in meeting with Penny's classmates since they were all in their seventies at that point. I stopped at the vacant hotel where Penny and Helen had lived and ate lunch while sitting on the back steps. I loved lingering there and walking the paths Pen would have walked countless times as a child and teenager. This was the beginning of the ritual to stop in Forrest for a couple of hours every time I passed through Illinois on my way to and from Florida.

Part III
Reflecting on life

Time and space have given me the gift of perspective, even though I continue to miss Penny. Without her presence, it is harder to imagine a rich and fulfilling life, yet love and memories support me.

After I began dating Penny, I soon realized that we had a lot in common: a love of nature, good and compatible senses of humor, an interest in spirituality, compassion for the underprivileged and defenseless, an interest in and appreciation of music and the arts and solid, Midwestern ethical values. But Penny was light years ahead of me. In some ways, I had lived my life superficially. Lacking in self-confidence, I armed myself with an undergraduate degree and two advanced degrees. As an educated, tall, White Anglo Saxon Protestant, I had built-in advantages. I was also very responsible; yet, in many ways, I was just a "suit." I had the image, but lacked substance. I did not live life authentically, but more as a chameleon.

I needed to explore how to live more fully. First, while I had the capacity to connect deeply, I didn't know the steps to achieve that goal. Secondly, I didn't know my true self. Loving Penny helped me to set boundaries of what was best for me, to believe in my abilities, and to trust my decisions.

Part IV
Connecting and loving deeply

Penny and I connected and loved deeply. Connecting referred to a degree and quality of interaction that was different from loving. Couples can love each other without connecting deeply. Although we did not use the word connecting, it is useful in describing our relationship. It meant sharing one's innermost feelings and completely sharing intellectual, emotional, and physical intimacy. It meant communicating openly, by apprising the other of every aspect. It also meant choosing to be with the other over spending time with relatives, friends or in social gatherings. Of course there were urgent matters that did take priority. Yet, for us, those were exceptions as we considered our time together to be a priority.

Except for our individual workouts, we spent virtually all of our free time together. We always held hands, not needing much outside stimulation such as concerts, plays, or movies. The excitement in our life was our love for each other.

Early in our relationship, I learned that connecting and loving deeply was Penny's expectation. More than that, it was a requirement for our relationship. The first change I noticed was that Penny expected to spend Saturday mornings together. In a former life, this had been my time to do yard work or complete routine maintenance. Grudgingly, I gave it up. Looking back, I realized how precious those mornings had become— times when we "hung out" together, sometimes going out to purchase something we needed or to window shop.

Those glorious years passed too quickly. I wanted to believe that we would last forever, yet everything has a season, a beginning and an end. And, at our end, we will come to our beginning. Penny wrote about that search. It is part of the natural order of the universe. It is better to have loved deeply and be cut short by fate than never to have loved at all.

David and Penny

Part V
Setting true boundaries

Penny taught me to set true boundaries largely by example. She could have thought of herself as a victim, given her abandonment issues and life-threatening cancer, yet she would not allow herself to pursue that direction. Completely authentic, she knew she could rise above those circumstances and redirect her life.

She used dance therapy with patients to illustrate what it meant to be a victim: allowing, sometimes even preferring, self-suffering because of life's events or viewing life as a series of excuses for which the injured party claims no responsibility. Her favorite phrase--"There's no place to go from there"--described victims.

In the early years of my marriage to Penny, I was very much a work in progress. I grew up with a father whose bad temper often frightened me and my family members. I was afraid of anger. Because of this, it was difficult for me to be direct with my feelings of frustration and anger, and I often reacted with passive-aggressive behavior. Penny would have none of it. Her insistence, although frustrating, showed me a better way to respond within positive boundaries that were right for me.

I also learned that Penny expected to be protected. We had hired a lawn care company in Sarasota to keep our property mowed and pruned. Unhappy about the workers' attention to details, Penny complained to the owner, a female, who was very rude to her. I didn't feel the incident concerned me, a testimonial to my conflict-avoider personality. Penny let me know that she was very unhappy that I didn't stand up for her and confront the owner about her disrespectful behavior. Penny's reprimand made me feel very small, and, going forward, I vowed to defend her point of view. I began to understand the value of taking care of the emotional side of loved ones and also the empowerment of taking care of myself.

Part VI
Finding purpose

Engaging in life was an antidote for my loneliness and it helped me deal with my grief. Nothing compensated for the void, yet having a schedule, being accountable, and running helped. The best overall antidote for grief was to find a new purpose in life. On the day of Penny's memorial service, I made the decision to write a narrative to honor her. Although it took a couple of years before I actually started to write it, I looked forward to interviewing people who knew Penny. As it turned out, the original writing of this tribute became a gift to me because it gave me purpose and a lot of work to do.

Once again, with the peak of Minnesota fall colors past, and the dreary months of November and December approaching, I took my cat, Samantha, who loved to travel, and drove to Sarasota. I wasn't sure what this location could offer, other than a respite from the cold. I simply would be open and wait. My answer came soon enough.

Penny and I had a long-standing interest in the rescue and rehabilitation of injured wildlife. I decided to check into the status of Pelican Man's Bird Sanctuary, one of our favorite places. It had closed after the death of its founder, Dale Shields. Later, after numerous appeals to the City of Sarasota to re-open, a number of rehabilitators had been rejected. Not Lee Fox. As I arrived at the site of the sanctuary, I was happy to see that Lee and her non-profit, Save Our Seabirds (SOS), were in full operation. After a congenial conversation, I volunteered to work as a groundskeeper and receptionist. Ultimately, I became a board member. Yet it was my responsibilities as bird rescuer that were the most rewarding. I was pleased to have another purpose in life.

Part VII
Enjoying humor

It was so much fun to be with Penny because she shared my perspectives on humor. It didn't matter if we were in a crowd of people or if it was just the two of us on our back deck. Of course, the greater the number of people around us, the greater the shock factor. Penny *loved* the possibilities of playful risk. Humorous banter was good for the soul, not to mention the relationship. Penny taught me to lighten up. She worked to make me laugh, and I retorted in-kind.

Sometimes I light-heartedly annoyed Penny in a public setting. She had the ultimate power in this situation because if I didn't stop, she would threaten to yell the "f" word, followed by the name of my workplace. I would push it to the point that she would start to say the word and then always give in.

During another humorous moment, I was meticulously sorting blueberries, placing in a separate pile those that did not meet with my standard of quality. Penny saw what I was doing and snatched the pile of blueberries that I had rejected. Eating them, she triumphantly made her point.

Part VIII
Finding enrichment as kindred spirits

For as long as I knew Penny, she had a keen interest in spirituality and listened to her intuition. She focused on the teachings of liberal Christian theologians and connected to her higher power through direct experience in nature. For each of us, nature was an important source of nurturance and inner strength. It also brought strength to our marriage. I believe that there is life beyond what we experience on this earth, perhaps in other dimensions. Our spirits survive death as evidenced by the owl that appeared outside the family room on the day after Penny died. This was a message from the spirit world. The presence of the owl meant that Penny was safe. I further believe that our spirits will meet at some future time.

As part of this reality, I continued to hope for more—for an appearance of Penny in some form, or an audible message or a sign of some kind. It wasn't long before my hopes were realized. I received another spirit world message.

Massage therapy helped to relieve my stress and release my grief. After several appointments, I learned that my massage therapist in Florida was also an intuitive. She told me that Penny was present and that she was joyful and very proud of me. Penny wanted to connect with me, yet did not want to hold me back. The therapist said she could feel tremendous love coming from Penny, and that I should be open to communication from her. I would feel, rather than think, the connection. After that, the therapist stated that there was "something about the bird feeder." This comment shocked me. She didn't know that I had a bird feeder in Minnesota, let alone its significance. The bird feeder hung from the same branch on which the owl perched the day after Penny died. Of course, I was very pleased to hear these messages.

Another acquaintance and SOS supporter also worked with energy healing. During my intuitive session with her, she confirmed Penny's presence and intense love. The healer was moved to tears as she said that there were no words to adequately describe Penny's love for me. Again, I felt uplifted and believed her messages to be credible.

I met with yet a third gifted medium who knew only that I had lost my wife to cancer. This practitioner indicated that Penny's cancer was in her lower abdomen and accurately confirmed a number of other facts about my life. She ended the session by saying that Penny would use feathers to communicate with me.

Upon returning to Minnesota, I began to find feathers over a period of about a month. One of the first feathers was located in the middle of the front door to my house, inside the outer screen door. Then there were two beautiful owl feathers in my driveway and two more on my running path. An unusually large owl feather was on the side of the road opposite my driveway. Each time I found a feather, I would say out loud, "Thank you, Penroe. Thank you, Penroe!" Then, as suddenly as it had begun, the appearance of feathers stopped.

I felt like I didn't need further confirmation. Penny was out there, somewhere in a different dimension. We are soul mates and will be together again in some way in the future. I will continue to talk with her, telling her what day it is, how long it has been since she left this earth plane, what is happening, and how much I love her. I have immense gratitude for the precious time we spent together. A friend gave me this quote from Thornton Wilder.

> "All that we can know about those we have loved and lost is that they would wish us to remember them with a more intensified realization of their reality. What is essential does not die, but clarifies. The highest tribute to the dead is not grief, but gratitude."

Part IX
Showing compassion for life

Penny and I were in awe of nature's beauty and the complexities of creation. We saw these things as evidence of a higher power and went out of our way to help our animal friends. We regularly stopped to assist turtles and other animals crossing the road; remodeled our home to enjoy the birds, squirrels, deer and wild turkeys that claimed the feeders; and fed a raccoon family that lived in a huge maple tree in our front yard.

Of even greater importance than supporting the abundant wildlife on our property were the animals we had tamed. Penny taught me not to get angry when our cats misbehaved, but rather to understand and work with them to correct the behavior that needed changing. Like people, cats have unique personalities. Samantha, a feisty, female orange tabby, shares my home. I work to accept her as she is and win her affection. In her cat-like ways, she makes clear her love for me.

Penny was highly passionate about the issue of animal welfare. Her love of animals began at an early age with her beloved dog, Gussie, and the white mare belonging to school friend, Kay Lindenbaum Crane. Penny would have loved the following nature passage:

> "For the animal shall not be measured by man. In a world older and more complete than ours they move finished and complete, gifted with extensions of the senses we have lost or never attained, living by voices we shall never hear. They are not brethren, they are not underlings; they are other nations, caught with ourselves in the net of life and time, fellow prisoners of the splendour and travail of the earth."
>
> THE OUTERMOST HOUSE A Year of Life on the Great Beach of Cape Cod[2]
> Henry Beston

Part X
Appreciating music and the arts

Penny believed that music and the arts expressed the values of beauty, sensitivity, and enrichment for those who took time to engage in those values. Through Penny's experience with the arts and her intuition and depth of understanding, she exposed me to greater awareness and appreciation of the arts. We both enjoyed playing music and singing. Music and the arts deepened our relationaship and gave us another way to connect. I developed a greater appreciation for celebrated composers and an understanding of art forms such as modern dance and opera.

Part XI
Finding meaning in life

As I continue my journey without Penny, it feels as if I am living only a shell of what my life once was. I continue to find ways to make a difference for others. In that way, I will attract people and situations that offer a more profound essence that satisfies me. Being in nature is another remedy for my emptiness. Even though people frequently disappoint me, nature rarely does.

A recent kayak trip to the Lower Brule River in northwestern Wisconsin spoke to me after I navigated a particularly challenging set of rapids. Although I capsized three times during the trip, I felt exhilaration, accomplishment, and zest for life. Only a temporary respite from my emptiness and not terribly practical on a regular basis, the adventure was still a source of much joy and happiness.

I am grateful for health, and running has been an essential part of my life. Shortly after turning seventy, I participated in the Park Point Five-Miler, the oldest running race in northern Minnesota. Singing and playing piano and guitar enrich my daily routine.

I am thankful for the experiences of my life and for the love of all relationships, especially for the one with Penny, the love-of-my-life. My foundation is strong, and I am filled with goodness and appreciation. Not knowing what will come, I am content to draw on strength and love, gifts from Penny.

Do you,
like the deer,
leave fresh tracks
in the snow

or a mark
where the cardinal
has perched
or the flame of a wing

in the woods?
What sound
or footfall
for a human ear?
Are the ears
to hear you in my hands,
the heart to love you
in my eyes?

Christmas Collection
2002

What sound or footfall for a human ear?

Notes

Letter to Readers

1. Reverend Wes Wasdyke was the priest referenced in *Christmas Collection, 2007*. Penny liked Wes and once gave him a hard copy of *Thirst,* by Mary Oliver, in appreciation for his presence in our lives.

Chapter 1: My Pen and Our Love

1. "God's eye," last modified August 24, 2014, en.wikipedia.org/wiki/God's_eye.

2. "Monarch Butterfly Danaus plexippus," accessed October 1, 2014, animals.nationalgeographic.com/animals/bugs/monarch-butterfly/.

3. Excerpts from THE LITTLE PRINCE by Antoine de Saint-Exupery, translated from the French by Richard Howard. Copyright 1943 by Houghton Mifflin Harcourt Publishing Company. Copyright (c) renewed 1971 by Consuelo de Saint-Exupery, English translation copyright ©2000 by Richard Howard. Reprinted by permission of Houghton Mifflin Harcourt Publishing Company. All rights reserved.

Chapter 2: Penny's Quest

1. Reverend Dr. James R. Newby, "Penny Bosselmann Memorial Message," (January 19, 2008), 1, lines 12-19, quoting Rainer Maria Rilke, *Letters to a Young Poet*, Letter 4; July 16, 1903; translator MD Herter Norton (New York: W.W. Norton), 33-34.

2. Excerpt from "Little Gidding" from FOUR QUARTETS by T.S. Eliot. Copyright 1940 by Houghton Mifflin Harcourt Publishing Company; Copyright (c) renewed 1968 by T.S. Eliot. Reprinted by permission of Houghton Mifflin Harcourt Publishing Company. All rights reserved.

Chapter 4: Forrest Memories

1. "Hollyhock Dolls + Easy How-to," last modified September 26, 2011, www.designmom.com/2011/09/hollyhock-dolls-easy-how-to.

2. The Korean War is known as the Forgotten War because of its comparison in the U.S. to World War II.

3. A camp sponsored by the Young Women's Christian Association (YWCA) that was located in west central Michigan near Grand Rapids.

4. stealing

5. "Detasseling," last modified April 21, 2014, en.wikipedia.org/

wiki/detasseling.

6. "Gramophone record," last modified September 14, 2014, en.wikipedia.org/wiki/gramophonerecord.

7. "Ouija," last modified October 1, 2014, en.wikipedia.org/wiki/ouija.

Chapter 5: The Articulate Wind

1. ...My right eye sees nothing.
   After the hemorrhage, the doctor
       said, "The cells of your right eye
       have died."
   My blind child sat down
       silent as a stool in the office,
       then flailed his arms.
       knocking things over.
   I have not wanted this flailing child.
   "My Right Eye," excerpt, June 26, 1996.

2. "What we believe," last modified September 28, 2014, www.stluke.mn/about-us/what-we-believe.

3. "Wild Geese" from DREAM WORK, copyright ©1986 by Mary Oliver. Used by permission of Grove/Atlantic, Inc. Any third party use of this material, outside of this publication, is prohibited.

Chapter 6: Thin Places

1. ©Stephen J. Patterson, 1998, "THE GOD OF JESUS: THE HISTORICAL JESUS AND THE SEARCH FOR MEANING," Trinity Press International, by permission of Bloomsbury Publishing Inc.

2. Reverend Dr. James R. Newby, "Penny Bosselmann Memorial Message," (January 19, 2008), 3, lines 19-20.

3. THE HEART OF CHRISTIANITY by MARCUS J. BORG Copyright (c) 2003 by Marcus Borg. Reprinted courtesy of HarperCollins Publishers.

4. See note 3 above.

5. "Marian Chace," last modified January 23, 2014, en.wikipedia.org/wiki/Marian_Chace.

6. "Allied Health Profession: Dance Therapy," last modified April, 2005, www.healthpronet.org/ahp_month/04_05.html.

7. "Dr. Judith S. Kestenberg, 88, Studied Survivors of Holocaust," last modified January 21, 1999, www.nytimes.com/1999/01/21/nyregion/dr-judith-s-kestenberg-88-studied-survivors-of-holocaust.html.

Chapter 8: Rhythms in Time

1. Excerpts from TUESDAYS WITH MORRIE: AN OLD MAN, A YOUNG MAN AND LIFE'S GREATEST LESSON by Mitch Albom, copyright 1997 by Mitch Albom. Used by permission of Doubleday, an imprint of the Knopf Doubleday Publishing Group, a division of Random House LLC. All rights reserved. Any third party use of this material, outside of this publication, is prohibited. Interested parties must apply directly to Random House LLC for permission.

2. "A Prairie Home Companion with Garrison Keillor," accessed September 28, 2014, prairiehome.org.

Chapter 9: Old Love

1. Used by permission from OLD LOVE by Neal & Leandra copyright 1992 Uncle Gus Music.

2. "Official online home of 'The Great One,'" accessed October 3, 2014, www.jackiegleason.com/poorsoul.html.

3. My husband and I add a room
> on the south side of our house,
> a room of windows,
> high cedar ceilings,
> a fat, black stove.
> We look out on the seasons of the woods
> and the stars.

Journal entry, excerpt; Novemeber 30, 1995.

4. "Investment Valuation Ratios: Price/Earnings Ratio," accessed October 1, 2014, www.investopedia.com/university/ratios/investment-valuation/ratio4.asp.

Chapter 10: The Rare Gift

1. THE HOLY BIBLE authorized King James Version (New York: Harper & Row), 1952, Genesis 29-31, 45-50.

2. Excerpts from THE LITTLE PRINCE by Antoine de Saint-Exupery, translated from the French by Richard Howard. Copyright 1943 by Houghton Mifflin Harcourt Publishing Company. Copyright (c) renewed 1971 by Consuelo de Saint-Exupery, English translation copyright ©2000 byRichard Howard. Reprinted by permission of Houghton Mifflin Harcourt Publishing Company. All rights reserved.

Chapter 11: Deep Knowing: A Monologue

1. Written before Penny's medical diagnosis of May, 1999.
2. "On Death and Dying," accessed October 3, 2014, www.ekrfoundation.org/five-stages-of-grief/.
3. Fictitious name

Chapter 12: Chrysalis

1. Penny Bosselmann, "Place One Card in Each of 5 Places," referencing Yoko Ono's *Place One Card in Each of 5 Places*, Walker Art Museum Exhibit: "Ono, YES" (Minneapolis: April 15, 2001).
2. "Certified International Qigong Master Chunyi Lin," accessed October 3, 2014, www.springforestqigong.com/index.php/master-chunyi-lin.
3. Fictitious name
4. At a debriefing session after Penny's passing, Dr. Judson told David that patients always know when they are going to die.
5. From the volume *Evidence* by Mary Oliver, published by Beacon Press, Boston Copyright ©2009 by Mary Oliver, used herewith by permission of the Charlotte Sheedy Literary Agency, Inc.
6. "Love after Love" from COLLECTED POEMS 1948-1984 by Derek Walcott. Copyright ©1986 by Derek Walcott. Reprinted by permission of Farrar, Straus and Giroux, LLC.
7. "Derek Walcott," last modified October 2, 2014, en.wikipedia.org/wiki/Derek_ Walcott. Walcott is the recipient of the 1992 Nobel Prize in Literature and the 2011 T.S. Eliot Prize for his book of poetry, *White Egrets*.

Epilogue

1. LONESOME VALLEY, words from Public Domain
2. "Quote" from the book THE OUTERMOST HOUSE: A Year Of Life On The Great Beach Of Cape Cod by Henry Beston. Copyright ©1928, 1949 by Henry Beston. Copyright renewed by Henry Beston, 1956. Copyright renewed by Elizabeth C. Beston, 1977. Reprinted by permission of Henry Holt and Company, LLC. All rights reserved.

Photographs

David Bosselmann, Paul Krause, Shutterstock.com

The Authors

David Bosselmann

Barbara Krause

David Bosselmann, Penny's soul mate, husband and best friend made a decision to write her biography at her Memorial Service on January 19, 2008 as a way of honoring her. He had no idea it would lead him on paths of discovery, healing and ultimate transformation. David retired from his financial planning practice in December, 2010. He is an avid runner, hiker, kayaker, bird rescuer and nature enthusiast. He currently resides in Deephaven, Minnesota and Tucson, Arizona.

Barbara Krause has been involved with storytelling, both oral and written, for the last ten years. She began shaping and ghostwriting nonfiction works six years ago. A passion for becoming one with her client's voice, she is moved intuitively to seek creative and unusual storyboards. With sense and sensibility, she enhances meaningful writing with interviews and research. Well told stories bring about laughter and tears, the unforgettable pearls of a reader's collection. Contact Barbara@MakingWordsWork.biz or visit her website at www.MakingWordsWork.biz.